*Experimental Research in
The Psychology of Music: 10*

Studies in the Psychology of Music
Volume 10

EDWIN GORDON

General Editor

Consulting Editors: Henry Cady, music education, Ohio State University; A. N. Hieronymus, education, University of Iowa; Charles Leonhard, music education, University of Illinois; Robert Thorndike, psychology, Teachers College, Columbia University; Himie Voxman, music, University of Iowa.

Experimental Research in The Psychology of Music: 10

EDWIN GORDON

Editor

UNIVERSITY OF IOWA PRESS  IOWA CITY

Library of Congress Cataloging in Publication Data (Revised)

Gordon, Edwin, 1927–
　　Experimental research in the psychology of music.

　　(University of Iowa.　Studies in the psychology of music, v. 6–10)
　　Includes bibliographies.
　　1.　Music—Psychology—Addresses, essays, lectures.
I.　Title.　II.　Series: Iowa.　University.　Studies in the psychology of music, v. 6.
ML3830.I71　　vol. 6, etc.　　　　781'.1'5　　　　73–632181
ISBN 0-87745-018-8

University of Iowa Press, Iowa City, Iowa 52242
© 1975 by The University of Iowa. All rights reserved
Printed in the United States of America

CONTENTS

PREFACE vii

AN INVESTIGATION OF THE STABILITY OF MUSICAL
APTITUDE AMONG PRIMARY-AGE CHILDREN 1

Robert M. De Yarman

FOURTH-YEAR AND FIFTH-YEAR FINAL RESULTS OF A
LONGITUDINAL STUDY OF THE MUSICAL ACHIEVEMENT
OF CULTURALLY-DISADVANTAGED STUDENTS 24

Edwin Gordon

THE EFFECTS OF TONAL PATTERN TRAINING ON THE
PERFORMANCE ACHIEVEMENT OF BEGINNING WIND
INSTRUMENTALISTS 53

Carol B. MacKnight

AN EXPERIMENTAL ANALYSIS OF THE DEVELOPMENT
OF TONAL CAPABILITIES OF FIRST GRADE
CHILDREN 77

Philip H. Miller

AN INVESTIGATION TO DETERMINE WHETHER LEARNING
EFFECTS ACCRUE FROM IMMEDIATE SEQUENTIAL
ADMINISTRATIONS OF THE SIX LEVELS OF THE
IOWA TESTS OF MUSIC LITERACY 98

Thelma Volger

A SELECTED BIBLIOGRAPHY FOR 1973 182

PREFACE

Nearly half a century ago, Carl E. Seashore initiated the Studies in the Psychology of Music at The University of Iowa. Dean Seashore was astutely aware of the need for furthering experimental research in the psychology of music, and the publication of the series represented only one of his major contributions to this cause.

The immediate overwhelming acceptance of the Studies in the Psychology of Music has not diminished over the years in spite of the fact that the series had to be discontinued in the 1930s. It is with great respect for the visionary genius of Carl E. Seashore that I am carrying forth his work and have accepted the responsibility of reactivating the Studies in the Psychology of Music some twenty years after his death. The support of my professional colleagues in recognizing the particular importance of the dissemination of results of current experimental research studies in the psychology of music provided impetus for the publication, in 1967, of Volume V of the series and succeeding volumes.

Under the aegis of The University of Iowa, the Studies in the Psychology of Music will be published annually. It is anticipated that because of the interdisciplinary nature of the psychology of music, each yearly volume will comprise a set of experimental research studies bearing on music, education, psychology, measurement, and/or acoustics. Undoubtedly, the continued success of the series is in large part dependent on the extent to which worthy studies are contributed for publication.

Edwin Gordon

AN INVESTIGATION OF THE STABILITY OF MUSICAL APTITUDE AMONG PRIMARY-AGE CHILDREN

Robert De Yarman

INTRODUCTION

The nature of musical aptitude, its source and description, has been of interest to music psychologists and music educators for a number of years. They are aware that in order to be most effective and efficient, teachers must be able to identify and direct instruction to each child's individual musical aptitudes.

Edwin Gordon, author of *The Musical Aptitude Profile*[1] (hereafter referred to as *MAP*) stresses, in the *MAP* Manual, the pedagogical need to identify and teach to each child's individual musical aptitude. In the *MAP* Manual, under "Interpretation and Use of Test Scores," Gordon includes specific teaching techniques intended to help music educators teach to children's different musical aptitude levels.

MAP was designed and standardized for students in fourth grade through twelfth grade. Therefore, the administration of *MAP* and the suggested techniques for teaching to students' various levels of musical aptitude are not directly applicable to children of third grade age and younger. Interested in the need to identify the musical potential of younger children, Harrington developed a *Primary Level MAP* intended for use with second and third grade children.[2] Using the exact music from only three subtests of the standard *MAP* (*Tonal Imagery — Melody*, *Rhythm Imagery — Tempo*, and *Musical Sensitivity — Phrasing*), Harrington tape recorded new test directions and developed multi-colored answer sheets. In his findings he reported relatively low (as compared to the standard *MAP*) Composite reliability coefficients.

Based upon Harrington's study, Gordon indirectly concluded, ". . . musical aptitude fluctuates throughout the primary grades . . . ."[3] Gordon's contention that musical aptitude fluctuates throughout the primary grades is based upon the low *MAP* Composite reliability coefficients reported by Harrington for second and third grade children. That is, referring to the high reliability coefficients in previous research with *MAP* with fourth grade children and older,[4,5,6,7] Gordon inferred that Harrington's findings of low *MAP* Composite reliability coefficients were due to the unstableness of young children's musical aptitude.

This conclusion became suspect, however, after De Yarman reported, in later research, relatively high *MAP* Composite reliability coefficients for children in kindergarten and first grade.[8] De Yarman's research included the use of an experimental version of Harrington's *Primary Level MAP* which he administered to children in kindergarten and first grade.[9] De Yarman used the exact music from the same three *MAP* subtests which Harrington used in his version of *MAP*. However, De Yarman developed different answer sheets and adapted Harrington's recorded test directions.

Although De Yarman's research was not concerned primarily with investigating the reliability of *MAP*, the *MAP* Composite reliability coefficients which he reported for children in kindergarten and first grade are higher than those reported by Harrington for children in second and third grades, and only slightly lower than the standard *MAP* Composite reliability coefficients reported for students in grades four, five, and six in the *MAP* Manual. It should be emphasized that the Composite test reliability coefficients for Harrington's and De Yarman's experimental versions of *MAP* are based on results of only three subtests rather than on the results of all seven subtests which comprise the standard *MAP*.

The discrepancies between Harrington's findings of relatively low *MAP* Composite reliability coefficients reported for second and third grade age children and De Yarman's findings of relatively high *MAP* Composite coefficients reported for even younger children, kindergarten and first grade age, are probably accounted for in the process validity and construct validity of the two adapted primary versions of *MAP*. A comparative analysis of Harrington's *Primary Level MAP* and De Yarman's experimental *Primary Level MAP* indicate that perhaps Harrington's version was not appropriate for use with second and third grade children. It appears that Harrington's multi-colored answer sheet and his adapted test directions were too difficult for most second and third grade age children to comprehend.

Another salient point is that Gordon states ". . . level of musical aptitude is influenced greatly by early exposure to music . . . ."[10] This inference regarding young children is derived from substantial and direct research with fourth grade age students and older. That is, because ". . . the *Musical Aptitude Profile* scores of both fourth-grade students and older students remain stable even after they have been exposed to musical practice and training,"[11] and due to the discrepancies between Harrington's and De Yarman's findings, Gordon's previous conclusion regarding the unstableness (as a result of the influence of practice and training) of young children's musical aptitude becomes questionable and requires further investigation and clarification based upon more direct and objective research.

Based upon the assumptions that musical aptitude is stabilized by at least age ten, approximately the fourth grade, and that aptitude is not influenced by musical practice and training (objectively substantiated at least with fourth grade students and older), the following study was undertaken in order to acquire additional, but objective, data regarding the nature of musical aptitude of primary age children. Of most interest was the age at which a child's level of musical potential is stabilized and the effects of early formalized music instruction on musical aptitude.

The results notwithstanding, this study has extremely important pedagogical implications. If, for example, succeeding fourth grade student's musical aptitude scores change significantly from year to year, then educators and music psychologists would have some objective evidence to support the assumption that pre-fourth grade formal music instruction does affect children's over-all potential to achieve. This would be of especial importance if the changes could be related directly to the amount and type of formal music instruction which children receive during the four years prior to entering the fourth grade. Conversely, if musical aptitude norms do not change significantly from year to year, that amount and type of formal music instruction which children receive during the four years prior to entering the fourth grade appear to have little effect upon children's over-all potential to achieve in music, then music psychologists and educators should be interested, pedagogically, to identify (objectively measure) and teach to each child's individual musical aptitude as soon as possible after beginning formal education. The main problems of this study were to investigate the following questions:

(1) Does musical aptitude stabilize before grade four (or age ten)?
(2) Do the effects of different amounts and types of formal music instruction before the fourth grade influence children's level of musical aptitudes (tonal imagery, rhythm imagery, and musical sensitivity)?

Subjects

The study included 2,980 children enrolled in the public schools of the Iowa City Community School District, Iowa City, Iowa. These children constituted four separate fourth grade classes from September 1968 through June 1972. In the first year of the study, 1968–69, 780 fourth grade children were administered *MAP*. In the following three years, 1969–70, 1970–71, and 1971–72, the same musical aptitude test was administered to 800, 800, and 600 children, respectively.[12] For purposes of this study, the children who were tested during the 1968–69 academic year will be referred to as Group I; and, those who were tested in the subsequent three years, 1969–70, 1970–71, and 1971–72, will be referred to as Group II, Group III and Group IV, respectively.

School Music Instruction
Group I

Fourth grade students who were administered *MAP* during the 1968-69 school year (Group I) received music instruction the first year of school from their regular kindergarten classroom teacher several times a week. In the subsequent three years, the children received instruction from a music specialist once a week for thirty minutes followed by two twenty-minute lessons each week from their regular classroom teacher. Beginning with their fifth year in the public schools (fourth grade), the children were exposed to a new music program which included instruction twice a week, twenty minutes each, from a music specialist. These children received approximately six months instruction in the new program before the aptitude test was administered to them.

Group II

Fourth grade students who were administered *MAP* during the 1969-70 school year (Group II) received music instruction the first year of school from their regular kindergarten classroom teacher several times a week. In the following two years, first grade and second grade, the children received instruction from a music specialist once a week for thirty minutes followed by two twenty-minute lessons each week from their regular classroom teacher. Beginning with their fourth year in the public schools (third grade), the children were exposed to a new music program which included instruction twice a week, twenty minutes each, from a music specialist. These children received approximately one year and two months instruction in the new program before the aptitude test was administered to them.

Group III

Fourth grade students who were administered *MAP* tests during the 1970-71 school year (Group III) received music instruction the first year of school from their regular kindergarten classroom teacher several times a week. In the following year, first grade, the children received instruction from a music specialist once a week for thirty minutes followed by two twenty-minute lessons each week from their regular classroom teacher. Beginning with their third year in the public schools (second grade), the children were exposed to a new music program which included instruction twice a week, twenty minutes each, from a music specialist. These children received approximately two years and two months instruction in the new program before the aptitude test was administered to them.

Group IV

Fourth grade students who were administered *MAP* during the 1971–72 school year (Group IV) received music instruction the first year of school from their regular kindergarten classroom teacher several times a week. In the following year, first grade, the children were exposed to a new music program which included instruction three times a week, twenty minutes each, from a music specialist. These children received approximately three years and two months instruction in the new program before the aptitude test was administered to them.

As indicated, the children in all groups were exposed to two or three types of music instructional programs during their five years of formal music education (kindergarten through fourth grade) before *MAP* was administered to them. Students in Groups I, II, and III received instruction in three different programs and Group IV received instruction in only two of the programs. Following is a brief description of the three programs and the amount of time the students in each group were exposed to the programs.

The children in all four groups were given a traditional type of kindergarten music program taught by the classroom teacher. Generally, the program consisted of action songs with piano accompaniments, finger plays and passive listening to recordings.

Described below is the type of music instruction which Group I was exposed to for three years (first through third grades), which Group II was exposed for two years (first and second grade) and which Group III was exposed to for one year (first grade). Group IV did not receive any instruction in the following program.

In this instructional program, children were taught by both a music specialist and their classroom teacher. This arrangement was typical in the sense that the music specialist taught one thirty-minute lesson each week and the classroom teacher was to follow up with two additional lessons. While the music specialist did provide lesson plans, it is questionable how many classroom teachers were able to follow through. During a typical half-hour weekly lesson, the music specialist would introduce two or three new songs to the children. Because most of the instructional time was devoted to teaching new songs, very little time was allotted to helping children develop their aural/oral skills in music. That is, based upon examination of the general music curriculum guide of the district, there did not appear to be a sequentially outlined music instructional program, one which would guide teachers in developing children's tonal and rhythmic skills.

Described below is the new music program (officially adopted by the Board of Education, district-wide, beginning with the 1968–69 academic year) which Group I was exposed to for less than one academic year (fourth grade) before *MAP* was administered to them, and which Groups II, III, and IV were exposed to for one, two, and three complete academic years, respectively, before *MAP* was administered to them. In the new program, the instruction which the children received was exemplary in that it was directed toward developing their aural/oral and kinesthetic music skills. The following quote is taken from the "Introduction" of the 1969 edition of the *Iowa City Community School District Elementary General Music Curriculum Guide*.[13]

> The salient characteristic of this music program is that students are taught as individuals within a group situation. Because the primary purpose of this program is to meet the needs of each child, the actual ability of the child is considered as being of secondary importance to how well he achieves commensurate with his potential for attainment. The essence of the program is to develop children's various musical abilities by first evaluating their musical strengths and weaknesses; second, establishing objectives for the music program; and finally, solidifying adequate methods of instruction.
>
> . . . .
>
> In the program music literacy is developed sequentially. Concepts added at one level generally are sustained and expanded upon in succeeding levels.

Music objectives are organized sequentially in each of the following areas:

Voice Ranges, Tessituras and Voice Breaks
Rhythmic Concepts
Tonal Concepts
Harmonic Concepts
Aesthetic Creative-Interpretive Concepts

Additional pedagogical and administrative guidelines for teachers and administrators are included for the following areas:

Establishment and Implementation of Objectives (sample lesson plan)
Schedule and Class Size
Materials
Performance (Classroom, Assembly, and Public)
Evaluation

In the companion *Resource Guide*, appropriate teaching techniques, including suggestions for the use of rhythmic, melodic, and harmonic musical instruments, are presented for each of the objectives listed in the *Curriculum Guide*. A supplementary section describing a number of musical games is also included.

Evaluation of Musical Aptitude

As indicated, sometime after students entered the fourth grade, their level of music aptitude was objectively measured through the use of the *Musical Ap-*

titude Profile (*MAP*).[14] Each music specialist was responsible for testing his/her own students. Except for Group I, which was tested near the end of their fourth grade academic year (1968–69),[15] the other Groups (II, III, and IV) were tested within the first three months of their fourth grade academic year, 1969, 1970, and 1971, respectively. All answer sheets were machine scored.

Statistical Design and Analysis
MAP Test Scores

Scores from the seven subtests of *MAP* plus three total scores (*Tonal Imagery, Rhythm Imagery,* and *Musical Sensitivity*) and a Composite score for each group were used to determine and compare the levels of musical aptitudes of each of the four experimental groups (Groups I, II, III, and IV).

Factorial Analyses

In order to acquire information relevant to the comparative musical aptitudes of each experimental group, *MAP* standard score means and standard deviations were tabulated. Then, eleven separate two-dimensional factorial analyses (one for each of the *MAP* scores) were undertaken. The two factors were level of aptitude and experimental group. As illustrated below, the four experimental groups who received different amounts and types of pre-fourth grade formal music instruction constituted the treatments dimension of the design. To establish the levels dimension of the factorial design, test scores of the children within the four groups were separated into five levels according to percentile rank for each analysis in the following manner: first to ninth, tenth to twenty-fourth, twenty-fifth to seventy-fourth, seventy-fifth to eighty-ninth, and ninetieth to ninety-ninth.

The significance of children's mean aptitude differences corresponding to experimental groups and levels of musical aptitude was investigated. Using the .05 level of confidence, each of the eleven factorial analyses was examined for the presence of a significant interaction, simple effects, and main effects.

Results of the Study

The results of the analyses may be found in Tables 1 through 11. In each of these tables may be found the means, over-all means, and standard deviations for each of the four experimental groups for a given *MAP* test. Tables 1 and 2 include results for the two *Tonal Imagery* subtests; Tables 4 and 5 include results for the two *Rhythm Imagery* subtests; and, Tables 7, 8, and 9 include

Description of the Experimental Design
Experimental Groups

	I (Tested During 1968-69)	II (Tested During 1969-70)	III (Tested During 1970-71)	IV (Tested During 1971-72)
90-99				
75-89				
25-74				
10-24				
1-9				

Musical Aptitude Percentile Rank Levels

results for the three *Musical Sensitivity* subtests. Tables 3, 6, and 10 include results for total scores (*Tonal Imagery*, *Rhythm Imagery*, and *Musical Sensitivity*); and, Table 11 includes results for the Composite scores. Except for Table 9, each of the remaining ten tables indicate a significant interaction between experimental groups and aptitude levels. Considering the rather high reliability of *MAP* [16] and the relatively large number of subjects tested, these results are not surprising. It would seem that even a slight deviation of trends of mean score differences among groups and levels for any one of the eleven test scores could produce a statistically significant interaction. For summary purposes, Figure 1 is included to pictorially reveal total tests (*Tonal Imagery*, *Rhythm Imagery*, and *Musical Sensitivity*) and Composite mean score differences. It can be seen from Figure 1 that the statistically significant interactions reported in the total test and Composite tables are probably a result of both the magnitude and the direction of mean score differences.

Although statistically significant interactions were found, it is interesting to note in Table 11 that the largest mean score difference within any level was for the Composite (5.5 points) between Groups I and III for students falling within the first to the ninth percentile level. However, relatively small mean score differences among the groups were found for the remaining test scores, generally less than two standard score points for the extreme difference within each of the upper three aptitude levels and two to four standard score points for the extreme difference within each of the lower two aptitude levels.

A study of the main effects reveals several more important facts. It can be observed in Table 2 that the smallest mean difference (2.0) among subtests was found for Groups I and III for *Tonal Imagery-Harmony*. The largest mean difference (3.3) among subtests was reported in Table 5 for Groups I and III for *Rhythm Imagery-Meter*. Comparatively, as reported in the *MAP* Manual for fourth grade students, the standard error of measurement for the *Tonal Imagery-Harmony* and *Rhythm Imagery-Meter* subtests is 4.7 and 4.5, respectively.[17] Also reported in the *MAP* Manual, the range of standard scores for the *Tonal Imagery-Harmony* and *Rhythm Imagery-Meter* subtests for fourth grade students is thirty-seven points (twenty-six to sixty-two and twenty-five to sixty-one, respectively).[18] Considering the standard *MAP* data (standard error of measurement and range of standard scores) in conjunction with the data from the present study, it can be observed that (1) among all the analyses (subtests, totals, and Composite), the largest mean score difference between any two groups lies well within one standard error of measurement and (2) when results from only Groups II, III, and IV are studied,[19] the differences are even smaller, from .4 of one score point between Groups III and IV (Table 2, *Tonal Imagery-Harmony*) to 1.3 score points between Groups II and IV (Table 11, Composite) to 2.1 score points between Groups III and IV (Table 5, *Rhythm Imagery-Meter*). Of most importance, however, is the fact that the mean differences (both simple and main effects) among the experimental groups are unsys-

Table 1

Musical Aptitude Profile Standard Score
Tonal Imagery-Melody Means and Standard
Deviations for the Four Fourth Grade
Experimental Groups

MAP Percentile Ranks	I			II			Groups III			IV			Over-all Means
	M	S.D.	N	M	S.D.	N	M	S.D.	N	M	S.D.	N	
90–99	64.1	3.67	78	62.7	3.43	80	63.5	3.34	80	63.5	3.69	60	63.4
75–89	57.4	1.87	117	56.1	1.77	120	55.8	1.80	120	55.6	2.38	90	56.2
25–74	49.5	3.37	390	47.1	3.51	400	46.1	3.62	400	46.1	3.17	300	47.2
10–24	41.5	1.43	117	38.2	2.09	120	37.1	1.73	120	37.8	2.33	90	38.7
1–9	34.0	3.66	78	31.7	2.83	80	29.6	3.58	80	29.5	3.36	60	31.2
Over-all Means	49.3			47.2			46.4			46.5			

SUMMARY TABLE

	df	ms	F-ratio
Groups	3	1572.38	166.10*
MAP Levels	4	55812.71	5895.72*
Interaction	12	64.62	6.82*
Within cells	2960	9.47	

*Significant at the five per cent level. F_{05} (3,2960) 2.60. F_{05} (4,2960) 2.37. F_{05} (12,2960) 1.75

Table 2

Musical Aptitude Profile Standard Score
Tonal Imagery-Harmony Means and Standard
Deviations for the Four Fourth Grade
Experimental Groups

MAP Percentile Ranks	Groups												Over-all Means
	I			II			III			IV			
	M	S.D.	N	M	S.D.	N	M	S.D.	N	M	S.D.	N	
90–99	61.0	3.03	78	59.6	3.43	80	60.8	3.46	80	59.9	2.25	60	60.3
75–89	55.6	1.55	117	53.4	1.71	120	53.5	1.73	120	53.8	1.81	90	54.1
25–74	47.4	3.21	390	45.8	3.33	400	45.3	3.21	400	45.3	3.52	300	46.0
10–24	38.7	1.52	117	36.8	1.88	120	36.3	1.75	120	36.9	1.47	90	37.2
1–9	32.1	3.70	78	30.1	3.56	80	28.9	3.78	80	31.1	2.83	60	30.6
Over-all Means	47.0			45.1			45.0			45.4			

SUMMARY TABLE

	df	ms	F-ratio
Groups	3	696.08	80.94*
MAP Levels	4	49224.28	5723.90*
Interaction	12	28.73	3.34*
Within cells	2960	8.60	

*Significant at the five per cent level. F_{05} (3,2960) 2.60. F_{05} (4,2960) 2.37. F_{05} (12,2960) 1.75

Table 3

Musical Aptitude Profile Standard Score Tonal Imagery-Total Means and Standard Deviations for the Four Fourth Grade Experimental Groups

MAP Percentile Ranks	I			II			Groups III			IV			Over-all Means
	M	S.D.	N	M	S.D.	N	M	S.D.	N	M	S.D.	N	
90–99	61.8	3.32	78	60.1	3.64	80	61.5	3.32	80	61.0	2.90	60	61.1
75–89	55.4	1.37	117	53.7	1.17	120	53.6	1.82	120	53.6	1.68	90	54.1
25–74	48.5	2.81	390	46.7	2.89	400	45.8	2.80	400	45.9	2.90	300	46.7
10–24	41.7	1.45	117	39.1	1.31	120	38.1	1.58	120	38.7	1.47	90	39.4
1–9	35.0	3.37	78	32.7	2.70	80	31.1	3.63	80	32.6	2.70	60	32.9
Over-all Means	48.5			46.5			46.0			46.4			

SUMMARY TABLE

	df	ms	F-ratio
Groups	3	1056.67	153.87*
MAP Levels	4	41778.34	6083.70*
Interaction	12	38.44	5.60*
Within cells	2960	6.87	

*Significant at the five per cent level. F_{05} (3,2960) 2.60. F_{05} (4,2960) 2.37. F_{05} (12,2960) 1.75

Table 4

Musical Aptitude Profile Standard Score
Rhythm Imagery-Tempo Means and Standard
Deviations for the Four Fourth Grade
Experimental Groups

MAP Percentile Ranks	I			II			III			IV			Over-all Means
	M	S.D.	N	M	S.D.	N	M	S.D.	N	M	S.D.	N	
90–99	61.9	3.62	78	59.0	3.50	80	60.3	4.03	80	62.5	3.68	60	60.9
75–89	54.7	1.60	117	52.4	1.48	120	53.1	1.18	120	54.7	1.61	90	53.7
25–74	47.8	2.86	390	45.2	3.03	400	45.0	3.19	400	46.8	3.05	300	46.2
10–24	40.9	1.11	117	37.6	1.61	120	36.7	1.55	120	38.9	1.66	90	38.5
1–9	34.0	3.45	78	31.3	3.30	80	29.5	3.64	80	30.7	3.88	60	31.4
Over-all Means	47.9			45.1			44.9			46.7			

SUMMARY TABLE

	df	ms	F-ratio
Groups	3	1470.29	184.66*
MAP Levels	4	44989.09	5650.32*
Interaction	12	56.87	7.14*
Within cells	2960	7.96	

*Significant at the five per cent level. F_{05} (3,2960) 2.60. F_{05} (4,2960) 2.37. F_{05} (12,2960) 1.75

Table 5

Musical Aptitude Profile Standard Score
Rhythm Imagery-Meter Means and Standard
Deviations for the Four Fourth Grade
Experimental Groups

MAP Percentile Ranks	I			II			III			IV			Over-all Means
	M	S.D.	N	M	S.D.	N	M	S.D.	N	M	S.D.	N	
90–99	60.7	3.06	78	57.8	3.55	80	57.2	3.91	80	60.5	3.97	60	59.1
75–89	53.5	1.53	117	51.6	1.36	120	50.7	1.22	120	52.8	1.51	90	52.2
25–74	46.4	2.84	390	44.0	3.09	400	42.8	3.07	400	45.0	3.37	300	44.6
10–24	38.9	1.71	117	35.7	1.31	120	34.5	1.71	120	36.1	1.53	90	36.3
1–9	31.3	3.44	78	29.1	3.08	80	28.0	3.37	80	29.0	4.16	60	29.4
Over-all Means	46.2			43.6			42.6			44.7			

SUMMARY TABLE

	df	ms	F-ratio
Groups	3	1785.39	223.27*
MAP Levels	4	46530.48	5818.89*
Interaction	12	23.71	2.96*
Within cells	2960	72.32	

*Significant at the five per cent level. F_{05} (3,2960) 2.60. F_{05} (4,2960) 2.37. F_{05} (12,2960) 1.75

Table 6

Musical Aptitude Profile Standard Score
Rhythm Imagery-Total Means and Standard
Deviations for the Four Fourth Grade
Experimental Groups

MAP Percentile Ranks	I			II			Groups III			IV			Over-all Means
	M	S.D.	N	M	S.D.	N	M	S.D.	N	M	S.D.	N	
90–99	59.9	2.89	78	57.3	3.28	80	57.7	3.21	80	60.2	3.30	60	58.8
75–89	54.0	1.39	117	51.9	1.29	120	51.2	1.52	120	53.5	1.17	90	52.7
25–74	47.3	2.66	390	44.9	2.94	400	44.2	2.89	400	46.1	3.07	300	45.6
10–24	40.6	1.30	117	37.5	1.49	120	36.7	1.38	120	38.3	1.25	90	38.3
1–9	34.7	3.26	78	31.5	2.75	80	30.2	3.03	80	31.9	3.54	60	32.1
Over-all Means	47.3			44.6			44.0			46.0			

SUMMARY TABLE

	df	ms	F-ratio
Groups	3	1600.98	237.71*
MAP Levels	4	37769.49	5607.97*
Interaction	12	25.98	3.86*
Within cells	2960	6.73	

*Significant at the five per cent level. F_{05} (3,2960) 2.60. F_{05} (4,2960) 2.37. F_{05} (12,2960) 1.75

Table 7

Musical Aptitude Profile Standard Score Sensitivity-Phrasing Means and Standard Deviations for the Four Fourth Grade Experimental Groups

MAP Percentile Ranks	I M	I S.D.	I N	II M	II S.D.	II N	Groups III M	III S.D.	III N	IV M	IV S.D.	IV N	Over-all Means
90-99	60.8	3.92	78	60.3	3.85	80	59.0	3.25	80	61.5	3.69	60	60.4
75-89	53.9	1.52	117	53.0	1.49	120	52.5	1.46	120	54.5	1.89	90	53.5
25-74	46.6	3.09	390	45.4	3.38	400	45.0	3.17	400	46.2	3.38	300	45.8
10-24	39.0	1.66	117	37.3	1.14	120	36.3	1.82	120	38.1	1.55	90	37.7
1-9	31.5	3.80	78	30.3	4.42	80	28.1	4.61	80	30.1	4.66	60	30.0
Over-all Means	46.4			45.3			44.2			46.1			

SUMMARY TABLE

	df	ms	F-ratio
Groups	3	581.93	62.18*
MAP Levels	4	48125.16	5142.35*
Interaction	12	25.04	2.68*
Within cells	2960	9.36	

*Significant at the five per cent level. F_{05} (3,2960) 2.60. F_{05} (4,2960) 2.37. F_{05} (12,2960) 1.75

Table 8

Musical Aptitude Profile Standard Score Sensitivity-Balance Means and Standard Deviations for the Four Fourth Grade Experimental Groups

MAP Percentile Ranks	I			II			III			IV			Over-all Means
	M	S.D.	N	M	S.D.	N	M	S.D.	N	M	S.D.	N	
90–99	60.5	3.24	78	59.4	3.63	80	58.5	3.70	80	60.4	4.95	60	59.7
75–89	54.1	1.64	117	51.9	1.89	120	51.2	1.61	120	52.0	2.05	90	52.3
25–74	45.8	3.13	390	44.2	3.03	400	43.1	2.99	400	43.9	2.71	300	44.3
10–24	37.9	1.88	117	35.6	1.93	120	35.3	1.58	120	36.7	1.55	90	36.4
1–9	30.3	3.67	78	28.3	3.68	80	27.5	4.22	80	30.0	3.96	60	29.0
Over-all Means	45.7			43.9			43.1			44.6			

SUMMARY TABLE

	df	ms	F-ratio
Groups	3	985.62	116.52*
MAP Levels	4	49437.21	5844.58*
Interaction	12	22.66	2.68*
Within cells	2960	8.46	

*Significant at the five per cent level. F_{05} (3,2960) 2.60. F_{05} (4,2960) 2.37. F_{05} (12,2960) 1.75

Table 9

Musical Aptitude Profile Standard Score
Sensitivity-Style Means and Standard
Deviations for the Four Fourth Grade
Experimental Groups

MAP Percentile Ranks	I			II			III			IV			Over-all Means
	M	S.D.	N	M	S.D.	N	M	S.D.	N	M	S.D.	N	
90–99	59.2	3.72	78	57.9	3.05	80	57.2	3.80	80	58.8	3.37	60	58.3
75–89	52.5	1.30	117	51.2	1.52	120	51.0	1.49	120	53.0	1.34	90	51.9
25–74	45.8	3.10	390	44.2	3.23	400	43.6	3.21	400	45.1	3.39	300	44.7
10–24	37.8	1.81	117	35.9	1.71	120	35.1	1.60	120	37.3	1.52	90	36.5
1–9	31.4	3.14	78	29.2	3.31	80	28.9	3.55	80	31.1	3.20	60	30.2
Over-all Means	45.3			43.7			43.2			45.1			

SUMMARY TABLE

	df	ms	F-ratio
Groups	3	811.60	97.79*
MAP Levels	4	42797.80	5156.99*
Interaction	12	10.58	1.27
Within cells	2960	8.30	

*Significant at the five per cent level. F_{05} (3,2960) 2.60. F_{05} (4,2960) 2.37. F_{05} (12,2960) 1.75

Table 10

Musical Aptitude Profile Standard Score
Sensitivity-Total Means and Standard
Deviations for the Four Fourth Grade
Experimental Groups

MAP Percentile Ranks	I M	I S.D.	I N	II M	II S.D.	II N	III M	III S.D.	III N	IV M	IV S.D.	IV N	Over-all Means
90–99	55.5	3.95	78	52.9	4.57	80	55.1	2.72	80	56.7	2.73	60	55.1
75–89	50.6	3.57	117	50.2	3.71	120	49.8	1.17	120	51.6	1.10	90	50.6
25–74	46.1	4.33	390	44.5	4.70	400	43.9	2.52	400	45.3	2.58	300	45.0
10–24	40.9	4.34	117	39.1	4.50	120	37.4	1.26	120	38.7	0.99	90	39.0
1–9	35.5	4.62	78	34.8	4.61	80	30.8	3.75	80	33.7	3.22	60	33.7
Over-all Means	45.7			44.3			43.4			45.2			

SUMMARY TABLE

	df	ms	F-ratio
Groups	3	760.52	59.15*
MAP Levels	4	24212.17	1883.11*
Interaction	12	107.83	8.38*
Within cells	2960	12.86	

*Significant at the five per cent level. F_{05} (3,2960) 2.60. F_{05} (4,2960) 2.37. F_{05} (12,2960) 1.75

Table 11

Musical Aptitude Profile Standard Score
Composite Means and Standard Deviations
For the Four Fourth Grade
Experimental Groups

MAP Percentile Ranks	I M	I S.D.	I N	II M	II S.D.	II N	III M	III S.D.	III N	IV M	IV S.D.	IV N	Over-all Means
90-99	55.9	4.36	78	53.8	3.63	80	56.0	2.71	80	57.0	2.47	60	55.7
75-89	51.9	3.62	117	49.5	3.61	120	50.4	1.27	120	51.6	1.37	90	50.9
25-74	47.3	3.60	390	45.4	4.22	400	44.6	2.30	400	45.7	2.32	300	45.8
10-24	42.5	3.37	117	40.3	4.27	120	38.5	1.18	120	39.9	1.14	90	40.3
1-9	38.4	4.17	78	37.0	4.34	80	32.9	2.96	80	34.9	2.70	60	35.9
Over-all Means	47.2			45.2			44.5			45.8			

SUMMARY TABLE

	df	ms	F-ratio
Groups	3	1020.60	98.54*
MAP Levels	4	20683.99	1997.01*
Interaction	12	130.07	12.56*
Within cells	2960	10.36	

*Significant at the five per cent level. F_{05} (3,2960) 2.60. F_{05} (4,2960) 2.37. F_{05} (12,2960) 1.75

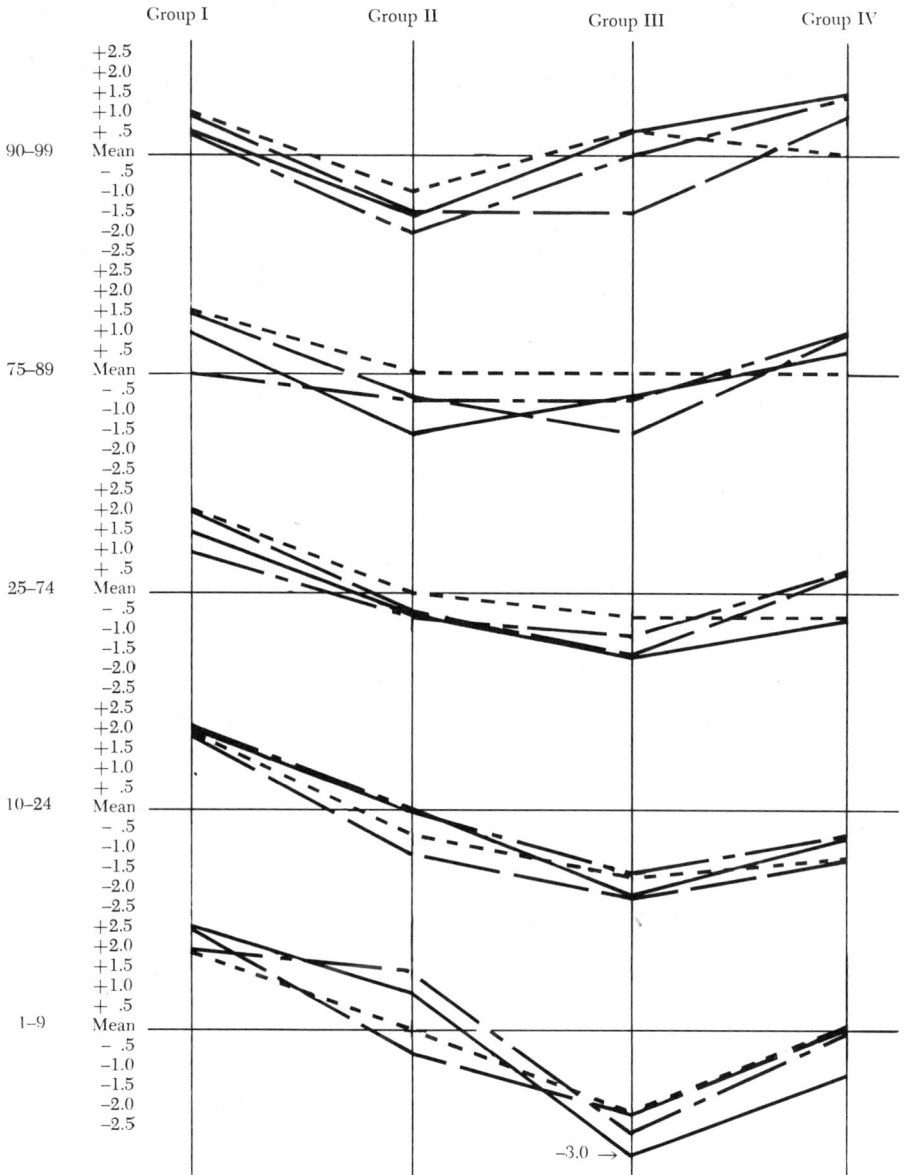

Figure 1. Interactions for Total Tests (Tonal Imagery, Rhythm Imagery, and Musical Sensitivity) and Composite

Tonal Imagery
Rhythm Imagery
Sensitivity
Composite

tematic, as described in Figure 1. Specifically, the largest positive mean difference between Experimental Groups I and IV is .6 standard score point for students at the ninetieth percentile rank and above on the *Rhythm Imagery-Tempo* subtest. Conversely, the largest negative mean difference between Experimental Groups I and IV is 4.5 standard score points for students below the tenth percentile on the *Tonal Imagery-Melody* subtest.

From a practical point of view, these comparative results dramatize the minimal extent to which different amounts and types of formal music instruction influence children's level of musical aptitudes before the fourth grade. That is, there is a lack of practical significance associated with the statistically significant interactions.

Conclusions

The results of the study objectively indicate that children's level of musical aptitude appears not to be influenced by early exposure to music — that neither type nor amount of formal music instruction before the fourth grade affects young children's level of musical aptitude. Further, it appears that musical aptitude stabilizes by at least age six (first grade), if not sooner. These objective results tend to corroborate De Yarman's earlier subjective findings (that musical aptitude probably stabilizes by kindergarten or first grade) and seriously questions published indirect conclusions that musical aptitude fluctuates (is unstable) among children in the primary grades (kindergarten through third grade).

Notes

Robert M. De Yarman is an assistant professor of music and education at the State University of New York at Buffalo.

    1   Edwin Gordon, *Musical Aptitude Profile* (Boston: Houghton Mifflin, 1965).

    2   Charles J. Harrington, "An Investigation of the Experimental Version Primary Level Musical Aptitude Profile for Use with Second and Third Grade Students," *Journal of Research in Music Education* 17 (1969):359–368.

    3   Edwin Gordon, *The Psychology of Music Teaching* (Englewood Cliffs: Prentice-Hall, 1971), p. 7.

    4   Edwin Gordon, *Manual: Musical Aptitude Profile* (Boston: Houghton Mifflin, 1965), pp. 58–79.

    5   Leon Fosha, "A Study of the Validity of the Musical Aptitude Profile" (Ph.D. diss., University of Iowa, 1960).

    6   Vernon Tarrell, "An Investigation of the Validity of the Musical Aptitude Profile," *Journal of Research in Music Education* 13 (1965):195–206.

    7   Edwin Gordon, *A Three-Year Longitudinal Predictive Study of the Musical Aptitude Profile*, Studies in the Psychology of Music, Vol. 5 (Iowa City: University of Iowa Press, 1967).

    8   Robert De Yarman, "An Experimental Analysis of the Development of Rhythmic and Tonal Capabilities of Kindergarten and First Grade Children," *Experimental Research in the Psychology of Music*, Studies in the Psychology of Music, Vol. 8 (Iowa City: University of Iowa Press, 1972), p. 15.

9 De Yarman, pp. 38–41.
10 Edwin Gordon, *The Psychology of Music Teaching*, p. 5.
11 Gordon, *Psychology of Music Teaching*, p. 5.
12 The total number of fourth grade children who were tested each year was slightly more than reported. However, in order to meet the requirement of proportionality in the design of the study, musical aptitude test scores of some students, for each year of the study, were randomly omitted.
13 Robert De Yarman, *Iowa City Community School District General Music Curriculum and Resource Guide* (Iowa City: Iowa Community School District, 1969).
14 For a detailed description of the *Musical Aptitude Profile*, see: Oscar K. Buros, editor, *The Seventh Mental Measurements Yearbook*, Vol. I (Highland Park: Gryphon Press, 1972), pp. 528–529.
15 Because it was the first year of the new instructional program, testing materials were not available to the music teachers until late in the 1968–69 academic year.
16 Edwin Gordon, *Manual: Musical Aptitude Profile*, p. 50 and p. 52.
17 Gordon, *Manual: Musical Aptitude Profile*, p. 52.
18 Gordon, *Manual: Musical Aptitude Profile*, pp. 90–91.
19 It is possible that the scores of students in Group I are generally higher than the scores of students in any of the other Groups because Students in Group I were tested late in their fourth grade academic year, as opposed to students in Groups II, III, and IV who were tested early in their respective fourth grade academic year.

BIBLIOGRAPHY

De Yarman, Robert M. "An Experimental Analysis of the Development of Rhythmic and Tonal Capabilities of Kindergarten and First Grade Children." *Experimental Research in the Psychology of Music*, Studies in the Psychology of Music, vol. 8. Iowa City: University of Iowa Press, 1972.

———. *Iowa City Community School District General Music Curriculum and Resource Guide*. Iowa City: Iowa City Community School District, 1969.

Fosha, Leon. "A Study of the Validity of the Musical Aptitude Profile." Ph.D. dissertation, University of Iowa, 1964.

Gordon, Edwin. *Manual: Musical Aptitude Profile*. Boston: Houghton Mifflin, 1965.

———. *The Psychology of Music Teaching*. Englewood Cliffs: Prentice-Hall, 1971.

Harrington, Charles J. "An Investigation of the Experimental Version Primary Level Musical Aptitude Profile for Use with Second and Third Grade Students." *Journal of Research in Music Education* 17 (1969).

Tarrell, Vernon. "An Investigation of the Validity of the Musical Aptitude Profile." *Journal of Research in Music Education* 13 (1965).

FOURTH-YEAR AND FIFTH-YEAR FINAL RESULTS OF A LONGITUDINAL STUDY OF THE MUSICAL ACHIEVEMENT OF CULTURALLY-DISADVANTAGED STUDENTS[1]

Edwin Gordon

In 1965, the Elementary and Secondary School Act, Title I, was established by the government of the United States. The purpose of this legislation was to provide financial aid to those schools classified as culturally-disadvantaged so that exiguous educational and cultural opportunities which are supposedly associated with such institutions might be mitigated. Current controversies notwithstanding, it was assumed that if students who attend culturally-disadvantaged schools were given educational opportunities similar to those accorded students who attend culturally-heterogeneous schools, the former group would at least more nearly achieve typical academic standards.

Particularly in regard to music education, there appears to be at least a logical basis for the foregoing assumption. Specifically, in a previous investigation (Gordon, 1967), it was demonstrated that potential (aptitude) for musical achievement is similar among groups of students who are classified as attending culturally-disadvantaged schools and those who are enrolled in culturally-heterogeneous schools. Unfortunately, of the 658 culturally-disadvantaged students who were identified in that study, only 13 of 55 who attained *MAP* (Gordon, 1965) composite scores above the 90th percentile participated in school music performance groups or performed on a musical instrument. Because only less than 25 per cent of the most musically talented students who attended the culturally-disadvantaged schools were given special instruction in music, an approximate inverse percentage to that found among a cross-section of students throughout the country (Gordon, 1965), the possibility of practicably further investigating the comparative extent to which culturally-disadvantaged and culturally-heterogeneous students achieve in music was precluded. Therefore, the purpose of this longitudinal study was to determine whether, if given similar educational opportunities, students who attend culturally-disadvantaged schools achieve in music at a level comparable to that of students who possess corresponding musical aptitudes but attend culturally-heterogeneous schools.

Design of the Study

In September 1968, MAP was administered to all fifth and sixth grade students in four culturally-disadvantaged elementary schools[2] (all in one junior and senior high school district) and three culturally-heterogeneous elementary schools (all in another junior and senior high school district) in Des Moines, Iowa. Then every student, regardless of his MAP scores, who volunteered to take instrumental music lessons and to participate in band activities for a five-year period was lent a relatively new musical instrument. The instruments provided (trumpets, cornets, trombones, saxophones, clarinets, and flutes) were donated to the University of Iowa by the National Association of Band Instrument Manufacturers for continuing research in the psychology of music. A substantial effort was made to allow students to study the instrument of their choice. The available instruments (230) were divided equally, according to type, between the two groups of schools.

The Des Moines Board of Education agreed to provide four highly-qualified instrumental music teachers to instruct the students.[3] Because of their declared interest and the type of teaching experiences they had had, two of the teachers were assigned to the culturally-disadvantaged schools and the other two teachers were assigned to the culturally-heterogeneous schools. During the initial years of the study, students received instrumentally-homogeneous group lessons each week as a curricular subject and each student was supplied with his own music. The musical content of the lessons was similar for all students but the musical progress of individual students was not dependent on the progress of the class as a whole. That is, the teachers taught to the students' individual musical differences as an integral part of the group lessons.

Just as soon as he was able, each student became a member of the school band and when appropriate, he participated in other musical activities. Each student was encouraged to enroll in the school summer band program. No student was discouraged from taking private instrumental lessons outside of school in addition to the regular group lessons provided in the schools. The teachers made every effort to motivate their students. To make the instructional process most effective, each of the teachers was given MAP results for every student in his group. A profile of each student's scores was plotted in his MAP Cumulative Record Folder by the teachers.

In September 1968, at the onset of this study, approximately 500 students were enrolled in the fifth and sixth grades of the seven participating schools; there were a few more than 250 in the four culturally-disadvantaged schools and fewer than 250 in the three culturally-heterogeneous schools. Of these, 82 in the culturally-disadvantaged schools and 96 in the culturally-heterogeneous schools initially volunteered to study instrumental music. Throughout the five years of the study, some students in each of the two cultural groups moved to new cities or from their respective school districts and in addition, the parents of some students in the disadvantaged group chose to have their children attend non-participating culturally-heterogeneous schools, and vice versa. Also, some students in both cultural groups chose to participate in work-study programs which were scheduled at the same time as the group lessons or music performance rehearsals. Therefore, the results of only 69 culturally-disadvantaged and 91 culturally-heterogeneous students were included in the analysis of the first year of the study, 60 culturally-disadvantaged and 72 culturally-heterogeneous students the second year, 54 culturally-disadvantaged and 57 culturally-heterogeneous students the third year, 40 culturally-disadvantaged and 40 culturally-heterogeneous the fourth year, and 28 culturally-disadvantaged and 35 culturally-heterogeneous the fifth year.[4]

As in the first three years of the study, the criteria used for evaluating students' musical achievement after four and five years of instruction consisted of ratings of their tape recorded instrumental etude performances and of their scores on the *Iowa Tests of Music Literacy*, Level 4 and Level 5 (Gordon, 1971). Levels 1, 2, and 3 of the *ITML* battery (which become sequentially more complex) are, of course, less complex than Levels 4 and 5, respectively. The three lower levels were administered to the students at the end of the corresponding first, second, and third years of the study. In similar fashion, the etudes which the students performed after one, two, and three years of instruction which were sequential in difficulty were less difficult than those which they performed at the end of the fourth and fifth years of the study, respectively.

The three etudes that the culturally-disadvantaged and culturally-heterogeneous students performed after the completion of four and five years of instruction were composed by the teachers, the content of the etudes being based on music contained in the students' methods book and other music they performed in band. The students prepared two etudes during the final four weeks of the fourth and fifth years of the study but the third etude was sight-read. Each year the three etudes were performed and recorded twice by each student, once during the penultimate week of school and again during the final week of school. The purpose for tape recording the etudes two times was to provide for an estimate of the test-retest reliability of the student's performances. (The fourth-year and fifth-year etudes, for all instruments, are appended to this report.)

Each student's performances were evaluated by two judges, both professors of music, to provide for an estimate of the inter-judge reliability of the ratings of the performances. The judges used a five-point rating scale to separately evaluate tonal, rhythmic, and expressive aspects of the students' performances. Thus, each year a student could earn up to 15 points from each judge for his performance of each etude and up to 90 points from each judge for both performances of all three etudes. Because students were identified only by a number and not by their name or school on the tape recordings, the judges were not aware whether they were evaluating the performances of a student attending a culturally-disadvantaged school or of a student attending a culturally-heterogeneous school. To ensure impartiality, the order of the students' performances on the tape recordings was different for each week.

The *Iowa Tests of Music Literacy* is a multi-level battery. Each of the six levels is comprised of two parts: *Tonal Concepts* and *Rhythmic Concepts*. Each part consists of three subtests which are titled *Aural Perception, Reading Recognition*, and *Notational Understanding*. As for the previous three years, only total scores on the *Tonal Concepts* and *Rhythmic Concepts* test and the complete *ITML* test served as achievement criteria for the fourth-year and fifth-year of the study.

In all, seven criteria of achievement were used each year: (1) the combined judges' ratings of both performances of the first prepared etude, (2) the combined judges' ratings of both performances of the second prepared etude, (3) the combined judges' ratings of both performances of the sight reading etude, (4) the combined judges' total ratings of both performances of the three etudes, (5) the *ITML Tonal Concepts* score, (6) the *ITML Rhythmic Concepts* score, and (7) the *ITML* composite score.

Each year the significance of the differences between the seven achievement means of the culturally-disadvantaged and the culturally-heterogeneous students was examined. This was accomplished through the use of a two-dimensional treatment by levels analysis; the two cultural groups represented the treatments, and high (above the 55th percentile[5]) and low (below the 55th percentile) *MAP* scores represented the levels. The analysis was completed seven times, once for each of the seven criteria. The effects of treatments and levels, and the interaction between these two factors, were studied.

Summary Review of the First-, Second- and Third-Year
Results of the Study

As indicated in previously published reports of the study (Gordon, 1970, Gordon, 1971; and Gordon, 1972), after one year of instruction, both the etude and *ITML* Level 1 treatment means significantly favored students who attend culturally-heterogeneous schools and the levels means significantly favored students with high musical aptitude regardless of their cultural status. The interaction effect was not found to be significant for any of the achievement criteria although the observed differences between the mean achievement of the culturally-heterogeneous and culturally-disadvantaged groups with low musical aptitude were consistently much greater (favoring the culturally-heterogeneous group) than the differences between the mean achievement of the culturally-heterogeneous and culturally-disadvantaged groups with high musical aptitude.[6] However, after two years of instruction, the differences between the etude treatment means for students who attend culturally-disadvantaged and culturally-heterogeneous were not significant although the observed means continued to favor the culturally-heterogeneous group. Similar to the first-year results of the study, *ITML* Level 2 treatment means were significantly higher for students who attend culturally-heterogeneous schools and for students with superior musical aptitude regardless of cultural background. And, no significant interaction effects were evidenced for any of the criteria the second year. The findings, after three years of instruction, were quite different from those for the first two years primarily because they were not uniform for all criteria. Like the second-year results, the differences between the means of the culturally-disadvantaged and culturally-heterogeneous groups for the first and second prepared etudes were not significant. However, unlike the results of the two previous years, the observed means favored the culturally-disadvantaged high aptitude group on these two criteria although the corresponding means continued to favor the culturally-heterogeneous low aptitude group. Nevertheless, the interaction effect for each of the two prepared etudes was not significant. Conversely, the levels effect for these two criteria (as for the other five criteria) was significant. The high aptitude students, regardless of cultural background, continued to demonstrate significantly higher achievement than low aptitude students. In regard to the analyses for the sight-reading etude and for all etudes combined, the interaction effects were significant. For these criteria, in contrast to the prepared etude criteria, the difference between treatment means for high aptitude culturally-disadvantaged and culturally-heterogeneous students (which favored the culturally-disadvantaged group) as compared to the difference between the treatment means for low aptitude culturally-disadvantaged and culturally-heterogeneous students (which favored the culturally-heterogeneous group) could not be attributed to chance. However, only the difference between the treatment means for low aptitude students for the sight-reading etude and all etudes combined was significant. Analogous to the results of the first and second years of the study, the treatment means for the *ITML* Level 3 *Tonal Concepts* test, the *Rhythmic Concepts* test, and the complete test significantly favored the culturally-heterogeneous students. And, again, the level effects for all *ITML* criteria (which favored the high aptitude student) were significant and the interaction effects were not.

Fourth-Year and Fifth-Year Results of the Study

The students who began instruction in the fifth and sixth grades in 1968 were enrolled in the eighth and ninth grade, and the ninth and tenth grade, respectively, during the fourth and fifth years of the study. Although the students no longer received group lessons, they were members of their junior high school or senior high school band throughout the last two years of the study. However, regardless of the school they were presently attending, the students performed the criterion etudes and took the appropriate Level of *ITML* at the conclusion of each of the final two years of study.

For the fourth and fifth years of the study, the reliabilities of the judges' ratings (as inferred from the correlations between their evaluations of students' tape recorded performances) are reported in Table 1 and the reliabilities of the students' performances (as inferred from the correlations between their first and second week recordings) are reported in Table 2. From an examination of Tables 1 and 2 it can be seen that, as for the first three years of the study, the reliabilities of the judges' ratings and reliabilities of the students' performance are substantial. The magnitude of these coefficients is similar to the split-halves reliability coefficients reported for Levels 4 and 5 of *ITML* in the test manual (Gordon, 1971). Specifically, with students in grades 7 through 9, the reliabilities of the *Tonal Concepts* test are .80 and .80, the *Rhythmic Concepts* test .84 and .85, and the complete test .90 and .91 for *ITML* Levels 4 and 5, respectively.

The fourth-year first prepared etude, second prepared etude, sight-reading etude, and the combined etude means, mean differences, and standard deviations for the students who attend culturally-disadvantaged and culturally-heterogeneous schools are presented in Tables 3, 4, 5, and 6, respectively. The summaries of the corresponding treatments by levels analysis of variance are also reported in these same tables.[7] In the same manner, the *ITML* Level 4 *Tonal Concepts* test, the *Rhythmic Concepts* test, and the composite test score means, mean differences, and standard deviations for these two groups of students are presented in Tables 7, 8, and 9, respectively, in conjunction with corresponding treatments by levels analysis of variance summaries.

Table 1

Correlations Between Judges' Evaluations of Students' Tape Recorded Instrumental Music Performances

	Fourth-Year	Fifth-Year
First Week		
First Prepared Etude	.95	.93
Second Prepared Etude	.94	.96
Sight-Reading Etude	.88	.89
Combined Three Etudes	.96	.96
Second Week		
First Prepared Etude	.95	.94
Second Prepared Etude	.95	.95
Sight-Reading Etude	.91	.92
Combined Three Etudes	.96	.97

Table 2

Correlations Between Students' Tape Recorded Instrumental
Music Performances on Two Adjacent Weeks

	Fourth-Year	Fifth-Year
Judge One		
First Prepared Etude	.82	.83
Second Prepared Etude	.86	.85
Sight-Reading Etude	.82	.84
Combined Three Etudes	.89	.90
Judge Two		
First Prepared Etude	.82	.83
Second Prepared Etude	.84	.84
Sight-Reading Etude	.81	.85
Combined Three Etudes	.87	.87

Table 3

Fourth-Year First Prepared Etude Means and Standard Deviations for
Students Who Attend Culturally-Disadvantaged and Culturally-
Heterogeneous Schools

	Culturally-Disadvantaged			Culturally-Heterogeneous			Mean Differences	Over-all Means
	Mean	S.D.	N	Mean	S.D.	N		
High MAP	48.8	5.89	20	41.0	9.52	20	7.8	44.9
Low MAP	44.2	9.76	20	35.8	8.35	20	8.4	40.0
Over-all Means	46.5			38.4			8.1	

Summary Table

	df	ms	F-ratio
Cultural Background	1	1304.11	17.08*
MAP Levels	1	475.31	6.23*
Interaction	1	1.51	0.02
Within cells	76	76.35	

*Significant at the five per cent level. F_{05} (1,76) > 3.98

Table 4

Fourth-Year Second Prepared Etude Means and Standard Deviations for Students Who Attend Culturally-Disadvantaged and Culturally-Heterogeneous Schools

	Culturally-Disadvantaged			Culturally-Heterogeneous			Mean Differences	Over-all Means
	Mean	S.D.	N	Mean	S.D.	N		
High MAP	43.3	81.0	20	39.9	10.10	20	3.4	41.6
Low MAP	39.9	9.45	20	32.4	8.10	20	7.5	36.2
Over-all Means	41.6			36.1			5.5	

Summary Table

	df	ms	F-ratio
Cultural Background	1	594.05	7.00*
MAP Levels	1	583.20	6.87*
Interaction	1	84.05	0.99
Within cells	76	84.88	

*Significant at the five per cent level. $F_{05}(1,76) > 3.98$

Table 5

Fourth-Year Sight-Reading Etude Means and Standard Deviations for Students Who Attend Culturally-Disadvantaged and Culturally-Heterogeneous Schools

	Culturally-Disadvantaged			Culturally-Heterogeneous			Mean Differences	Over-all Means
	Mean	S.D.	N	Mean	S.D.	N		
High MAP	42.3	8.03	20	38.5	7.57	20	3.8	40.7
Low MAP	39.0	7.73	20	32.5	6.43	20	6.5	35.5
Over-all Means	40.4			35.8			4.6	

Summary Table

	df	ms	F-ratio
Cultural Background	1	432.45	7.37*
MAP Levels	1	530.45	9.04*
Interaction	1	36.45	0.62
Within cells	76	58.69	

*Significant at the five per cent level. $F_{05}(1,76) > 3.98$

Table 6

Fourth-Year Composite Etude Means and Standard Deviations for Students Who Attend Culturally-Disadvantaged and Culturally-Heterogeneous Schools

	Culturally-Disadvantaged			Culturally-Heterogeneous			Mean Differences	Over-all Means
	Mean	S.D.	N	Mean	S.D.	N		
High MAP	134.4	20.80	20	119.4	26.15	20	15.0	127.1
Low MAP	123.1	25.31	20	100.7	21.73	20	22.4	111.6
Over-all Means	128.4			110.3			18.1	

Summary Table

	df	ms	F-ratio
Cultural Background	1	6606.61	11.26*
MAP Levels	1	4758.61	8.11*
Interaction	1	270.11	0.46
Within cells	76	586.67	

*Significant at the five per cent level. $F_{05}(1,76) > 3.98$

Table 7

Level Four *ITML* Tonal Concepts Standard Score Means And Standard Deviations for Students Who Attend Culturally-Disadvantaged and Culturally-Heterogeneous Schools

	Culturally-Disadvantaged			Culturally-Heterogeneous			Mean Differences	Over-all Means
	Mean	S.D.	N	Mean	S.D.	N		
High MAP	50.9	8.01	20	51.5	7.08	20	−0.6	51.2
Low MAP	51.6	7.55	20	53.5	8.02	20	−1.9	52.6
Over-all Means	51.3			52.5			−1.2	

Summary Table

	df	ms	F-ratio+
Cultural Background	1	31.25	0.50
MAP Levels	1	33.80	0.55
Interaction	1	7.20	0.12
Within cells	76	61.98	

+None are significant at the five per cent level. $F_{05}(1,76) > 3.96$

Table 8

Level Four *ITML* Rhythmic Concepts Standard Score Means
And Standard Deviations for Students Who Attend Culturally-
Disadvantaged and Culturally-Heterogeneous Schools

	Culturally-Disadvantaged			Culturally-Heterogeneous			Mean Differences	Over-all Means
	Mean	S.D.	N	Mean	S.D.	N		
High MAP	54.9	8.34	20	55.0	7.54	20	−0.1	55.0
Low MAP	51.3	8.99	20	48.3	6.75	20	3.0	49.8
Over-all Means	53.1			51.7			1.4	

Summary Table

	df	ms	F-ratio
Cultural Background	1	42.05	0.63
MAP Levels	1	530.45	7.98*
Interaction	1	48.05	0.72
Within cells	76	66.50	

*Significant at the five per cent level. $F_{05}(1,76) > 3.98$

Table 9

Level Four *ITML* Composite Standard Score Means
And Standard Deviations for Students Who Attend Culturally-
Disadvantaged and Culturally-Heterogeneous Schools

	Culturally-Disadvantaged			Culturally-Heterogeneous			Mean Differences	Over-all Means
	Mean	S.D.	N	Mean	S.D.	N		
High MAP	52.7	7.10	20	53.2	6.05	20	−0.5	53.0
Low MAP	51.3	6.50	20	50.8	6.27	20	0.5	51.1
Over-all Means	52.0			52.0			0.0	

Summary Table

	df	ms	F-ratio+
Cultural Background	1	0.01	0.00
MAP Levels	1	70.31	1.59
Interaction	1	5.51	0.12
Within cells	76	44.36	

+None are significant at the five per cent level. $F_{05}(1,76) > 3.96$

As can be seen in Tables 3, 4, 5, and 6, the means for each of the three etudes and the three etudes combined are significantly higher for students who attend culturally-disadvantaged schools than for students who attend culturally-heterogeneous schools. The over-all means for high aptitude students are significantly higher than the over-all means for low aptitude students on all etude criteria. The interaction effects, as indicated, are nonsignificant. However, it should be noticed that the observed mean for low aptitude culturally-disadvantaged students is higher (though nonsignificant) than the observed mean for high aptitude culturally-heterogeneous students for the three etudes combined, as shown in Table 6.

The analyses concerning *ITML* criteria are diverse. Neither mean differences for students in different cultural groups nor for students designated as possessing different levels of aptitude are significant for the *Tonal Concepts* or composite test scores. However, the negligible observed mean differences, as shown in Tables 7 and 9, favor culturally-heterogeneous students of both aptitude levels on the *Tonal Concepts* test but only high aptitude culturally-heterogeneous students on the composite test. Moreover, curiously, the negligible mean differences favor the low aptitude students in both cultural groups on the *Tonal Concepts* test. The observed (though nonsignificant) mean differences on the *Rhythmic Concepts* test favor the high aptitude culturally-heterogeneous students and the low aptitude culturally-disadvantaged students, as illustrated in Table 8. In contrast, high aptitude students, regardless of cultural background, scored significantly higher than low aptitude students on the same criterion. This significant result most probably gave rise to the slight observed mean difference on the composite test which favors low aptitude culturally-disadvantaged students. As for previous years, none of the interaction effects was found to be significant for the three *ITML* criteria.

A probable cause of the nonsignificant *ITML* tonal and rhythmic treatments effects and the nonsignificant (if not illogical) *ITML* tonal levels effect may be that following traditional practice, neither group of students was accorded sufficient training in general music classes or instrumental instruction to enable them to understand all of the concepts represented in the Level 4 *ITML* test. Specifically, half of the test items in the *Tonal Concepts Reading Recognition* and *Notational Understanding* subtests are written in the bass clef but only the trombone players were trained to read the bass clef. And, to a lesser extent, although approximately half of the items in the *Tonal Concepts Aural Perception* and *Reading Recognition* subtests are nontonal, the only instruction the students received in nontonal music was in connection with the Second Prepared Etude. The one apparent concern with the content of the *Rhythmic Concepts* test is that approximately half of the items in the *Aural Perception* and *Reading Recognition* subtests are in unusual meter (i.e., 5/8, 7/8, and 11/8). However, again in this case only by virtue of the First Prepared Etude, the students received at least some instruction in unusual meter. The suppositions that training in general music classes and instrumental music might not have been complementary and that the students might not have been extensively exposed to music in their classes and performance groups which included the concepts contained in *ITML* (their higher mean scores as compared to those for junior high school instrumental and noninstrumental music students combined who participated in the *ITML* national standardization program notwithstanding) is indirectly substantiated by the rather low correlations (considering the reliability of the criteria) reported in Table 10, between their etude performance ratings and their *ITML* scores. The lower correlations between their *ITML Tonal Concepts* test scores and their etude performance ratings as compared to the higher (and significant) correlations between their *ITML Rhythmic Concepts* test scores and their etude performance ratings are most probably attributable to the use of the bass clef, exacerbated by the presence of nontonal items, in the *ITML Tonal Concepts* subtests.

Table 10

Correlations Between Students' Scores on Level Four of *ITML* and Judges' Composite Evaluations of Their Fourth-Year Tape Recorded Instrumental Performances of the Three Criterion Etudes

	Tonal Concepts	Rhythmic Concepts	Composite Score
First Prepared Etude	.19	.35	.32
Second Prepared Etude	.15	.40	.32
Sight-Reading Etude	.08	.35	.25
Three Etudes Combined	.15	.39	.32

The fifth-year first prepared etude, second prepared etude, sight-reading etude, and the combined etude means, mean differences, and standard deviations for the students who attend culturally-disadvantaged and culturally-heterogeneous schools are presented in Tables 11, 12, 13 and 14, respectively. The summaries of the corresponding treatments by levels analysis of variance are also reported in these same tables.[8] In the same manner, the *ITML* Level 5 *Tonal Concepts* test, the *Rhythmic Concepts* test, and the composite test score means, mean differences, and standard deviations for these two groups of students are presented in Tables 15, 16 and 17, respectively, in conjunction with corresponding treatments by levels analysis of variance summaries.

Table 11

Fifth-Year First Prepared Etude Means and Standard Deviations for Students Who Attend Culturally-Disadvantaged and Culturally-Heterogeneous Schools

	Culturally-Disadvantaged			Culturally-Heterogeneous			Mean Differences	Over-all Means
	Mean	S.D.	N	Mean	S.D.	N		
High MAP	50.7	5.61	16	43.0	9.32	20	7.7	46.9
Low MAP	44.3	10.86	12	37.8	8.19	15	6.5	41.1
Over-all Means	47.5			40.4			7.1	

Summary Table

	df	ms	F-ratio
Cultural Background	1	804.76	10.80*
MAP Levels	1	513.03	6.89*
Interaction	1	5.04	.07
Within Cells	59	74.48	

*Significant at the five per cent level. $F_{05}(1,59) > 4.01$

Table 12

Fifth-Year Second Prepared Etude Means and Standard Deviations for Students Who Attend Culturally-Disadvantaged and Culturally-Heterogeneous Schools

	Culturally-Disadvantaged			Culturally-Heterogeneous			Mean Differences	Over-all Means
	Mean	S.D.	N	Mean	S.D.	N		
High MAP	45.0	8.32	16	41.0	10.04	20	4.0	43.0
Low MAP	41.1	10.30	12	34.6	8.07	15	6.5	37.9
Over-all Means	43.1			37.8			5.3	

Summary Table

	df	ms	F-ratio
Cultural Background	1	391.45	4.59*
MAP Levels	1	450.00	5.28*
Interaction	1	24.93	.29
Within Cells	59	85.26	

*Significant at the five per cent level. $F_{05}(1,59) > 4.01$

Table 13

Fifth-Year Sight-Reading Etude Means and Standard Deviations for Students Who Attend Culturally-Disadvantaged and Culturally-Heterogeneous Schools

	Culturally-Disadvantaged			Culturally-Heterogeneous			Mean Differences	Over-all Means
	Mean	S.D.	N	Mean	S.D.	N		
High MAP	44.3	8.62	16	40.0	8.07	20	4.3	42.2
Low MAP	39.9	7.67	12	33.5	6.40	15	6.4	36.7
Over-all Means	42.1			36.8			5.3	

Summary Table

	df	ms	F-ratio
Cultural Background	1	420.76	7.02*
MAP Levels	1	484.10	8.07*
Interaction	1	17.61	.29
Within Cells	59	59.96	

*Significant at the five per cent level. $F_{05}\,(1,59) > 4.01$

Table 14

Fifth-Year Composite Etude Means and Standard Deviations for Students Who Attend Culturally-Disadvantaged and Culturally-Heterogeneous Schools

	Culturally-Disadvantaged			Culturally-Heterogeneous			Mean Differences	Over-all Means
	Mean	S.D.	N	Mean	S.D.	N		
High MAP	140.0	21.34	16	124.1	26.27	20	15.9	132.1
Low MAP	125.3	27.35	12	105.9	21.45	15	19.4	115.6
Over-all Means	132.7			115.0			17.7	

Summary Table

	df	ms	F-ratio
Cultural Background	1	4715.01	8.03*
MAP Levels	1	4338.29	7.39*
Interaction	1	48.24	.08
Within Cells	59	586.82	

*Significant at the five per cent level. $F_{05}\,(1,59) > 4.01$

Table 15

Level Five *ITML* Tonal Concepts Standard Score Means
And Standard Deviations for Students Who Attend Culturally-
Disadvantaged and Culturally-Heterogeneous Schools

	Culturally-Disadvantaged			Culturally-Heterogeneous			Mean Differences	Over-all Means
	Mean	S.D.	N	Mean	S.D.	N		
High MAP	62.6	5.68	16	60.6	5.87	20	2.0	61.6
Low MAP	56.6	7.51	12	52.4	5.18	15	4.2	54.5
Over-all Means	59.6			56.5			3.4	

Summary Table

	df	ms	F-ratio
Cultural Background	1	137.15	3.80
MAP Levels	1	824.10	22.84*
Interaction	1	18.58	.51
Within Cells	59	36.08	

*Significant at the five per cent level. F_{05} (1,59) > 4.01

Table 16

Level Five *ITML* Rhythmic Concepts Standard Score Means
And Standard Deviations for Students Who Attend Culturally-
Disadvantaged and Culturally-Heterogeneous Schools

	Culturally-Disadvantaged			Culturally-Heterogeneous			Mean Differences	Over-all Means
	Mean	S.D.	N	Mean	S.D.	N		
High MAP	60.8	7.11	16	58.0	6.77	20	2.8	59.4
Low MAP	55.9	8.76	12	51.3	4.89	15	4.6	53.6
Over-all Means	58.4			54.7			3.7	

Summary Table

	df	ms	F-ratio
Cultural Background	1	203.26	4.31*
MAP Levels	1	538.87	11.42*
Interaction	1	11.72	.25
Within Cells	59	47.18	

*Significant at the five per cent level. F_{05} (1,59) > 4.01

Table 17

Level Five *ITML* Composite Standard Score Means
And Standard Deviations for Students Who Attend Culturally-
Disadvantaged and Culturally-Heterogeneous Schools

	Culturally-Disadvantaged			Culturally-Heterogeneous			Mean Differences	Over-all Means
	Mean	S.D.	N	Mean	S.D.	N		
High MAP	61.7	5.37	16	59.3	5.28	20	2.4	60.5
Low MAP	56.3	6.44	12	51.9	4.59	15	4.4	54.1
Over-all Means	59.0			55.6			3.4	

Summary Table

	df	ms	F-ratio
Cultural Background	1	170.48	5.90*
MAP Levels	1	657.22	22.73*
Interaction	1	15.88	.55
Within Cells	59	28.91	

*Significant at the five per cent level. $F_{05}(1,59) > 4.01$

As can be seen in Tables 11, 12, 13, and 14, the means for each of the three etudes and the three etudes combined continue to be significantly higher the fifth year for students who attend culturally-disadvantaged schools than for students who attend culturally-heterogeneous schools. And, like the fourth-year results, the over-all means for high aptitude students are significantly higher than the over-all means for low aptitude students for all etude criteria the fifth year. Although, again, the interaction effects were nonsignificant for all etude criteria the fifth year, the observed mean difference (though nonsignificant) for low aptitude culturally-disadvantaged students and high aptitude culturally-heterogeneous students for these criteria continues to favor, as shown in Table 14, the low aptitude culturally-disadvantaged group.

Unlike the results of the fourth year, the fifth-year results of *ITML* criteria are more consistent and uniform. As can be seen in Tables 15, 16, and 17, the means on the *ITML Rhythmic Concepts* test and on the composite test significantly favor the culturally-disadvantaged students and the means on the *ITML Tonal Concepts* test, although nonsignificant, also favor the culturally-disadvantaged students. Even more unlike the fourth-year results, the levels effects for all fifth-year *ITML* criteria are significant and as would be expected, the means favor the high aptitude students regardless of cultural background. The interaction effects, as indicated in these same tables, are nonsignificant.

The dissimilar results for the *ITML* criteria for the fourth and fifth years of the study are probably directly related to the comparative tonal content of Levels 4 and 5 of the test battery and to the extended instruction students received in unusual meter which relates to the rhythmic content of both Levels 4 and 5 of the test battery. Specifically, even though the students might not have received an abundance of instruction in nontonal music the fifth year, this, in and of itself, probably did not greatly affect the results of the analyses for the *ITML* Level 5 *Tonal Concepts* test because nontonal items are found only in the *Notational Understanding* subtest; the *Aural Perception* and *Reading Recognition* subtests include only two-part major and minor items. And, both the treble and bass clefs are used alternately in the *ITML* Level 5 *Notational Understanding* subtest whereas the bass clef is used exclusively in the *ITML* Level 4 *Notational Understanding* subtest. In this sense, it would seem that the *ITML* Level 5 *Notational Understanding* subtest should have better content validity for students who participated in this study because the majority of them had little or no exposure to the bass clef in their musical training. In regard to the analyses for the *ITML* Level 5 *Rhythmic Concepts* test, it, like the *ITML* Level 4 *Rhythmic Concepts* test, includes items in unusual meter. As a result of an additional year of instruction in unusual meter, the more capable students were able to demonstrate their significantly better skills on the *ITML* Level 5 *Rhythmic Concepts* test, but after only one year of exposure to these concepts, their skills were not developed adequately enough to produce significantly higher means on the *ITML* Level 4 *Rhythmic Concepts* test. This interpretation is indirectly substantiated by the comparison of the correlations between students' fifth-year etude performance ratings and their *ITML* Level 5 scores, presented in Table 18, with the correlations between students' fourth-year etude performance ratings and their *ITML* Level 4 scores which were reported in Table 10. All of the coefficients are significant in Table 18, but only the coefficients in conjunction with the *ITML Rhythmic Concepts* test are significant in Table 10. In this connection, it seems reasonable to assume that if the students had received instruction sequentially consistent with the content of the various levels of *ITML*, the trend of the results of the analyses for the *ITML* criteria over the five-year period of the study would have been as logical as the trend of the results of the analyses for the etude criteria throughout the course of the study.

Table 18

Correlations Between Students' Scores on Level Five of *ITML*
And Judges' Composite Evaluations of Their Fifth-Year Tape Recorded
Instrumental Performances of the Three Criterion Etudes

	Tonal Concepts	Rhythmic Concepts	Composite Score
First Prepared Etude	.28	.31	.35
Second Prepared Etude	.30	.35	.38
Sight-Reading Etude	.28	.30	.33
Three Etudes Combined	.29	.33	.40

In view of the fact that, for the fifth-year analyses, a significant difference was not found between the means for the culturally-disadvantaged group and the culturally-heterogeneous group on the *ITML Tonal Concepts* test, but it was evidenced for the remaining six criteria, a multivariate test of equality of mean vectors for all seven fifth-year criteria was undertaken. Considering that 6 and 54 degrees of freedom requires an F-ratio of 2.28 for significance at the five per cent level of confidence, both the cultural background factor (treatments) and the musical aptitude factor (levels) were found to be significant and, as expected, the interaction effect between these two factors was found to be nonsignificant. The F-ratio for treatments was 2.76; for levels, 4.58; and for interaction, 0.84. Succinctly, the results of the multivariate analysis indicate that when all seven criteria are combined and therefore considered as one criterion, the over-all mean differences significantly favor culturally-disadvantaged students and also students with high musical aptitude regardless of their cultural background.

Conclusions

From the continuing results of this longitudinal study it may be confidently concluded that if given appropriate compensatory instruction over a period of years, students who attend culturally-disadvantaged schools (although initially deficient) can ultimately surpass students who attend culturally-heterogeneous schools in musical achievement. This is true for both performance skills and cognitive abilities. Moreover, culturally-disadvantaged students who possess below average musical aptitude can ultimately achieve standards in musical achievement similar to those demonstrated by culturally-heterogeneous students who possess above average musical aptitude. However, overall, students with above average musical aptitude, regardless of cultural background, can better develop musical understandings than students with below average musical aptitude as identified by their scores on the *Musical Aptitude Profile*.

The far-reaching implications of these conclusions for music educators are: (1) that musically talented students can probably be identified among any group of students they might have the opportunity to teach, and (2) after students who can profit most from music instruction are identified, it is imperative that educators give adequate attention, by teaching to individual differences, to these students who are able to compensate for their meager background by achieving in a discipline in which success is not hampered by irrelevant factors that might be associated with one's past or present cultural background.

APPENDIX

PREPARED ETUDES

Fourth-Year
Trumpet, Cornet, and Clarinet

FIRST PREPARED ETUDE

SECOND PREPARED ETUDE

SIGHT-READING ETUDE

Fourth-Year
Flute

FIRST PREPARED ETUDE

SECOND PREPARED ETUDE

SIGHT-READING ETUDE

Fourth-Year
Saxophone

FIRST PREPARED ETUDE

SECOND PREPARED ETUDE

SIGHT-READING ETUDE

Fourth-Year Trombone

FIRST PREPARED ETUDE

SECOND PREPARED ETUDE

SIGHT-READING ETUDE

Fifth-Year
Trumpet, Cornet, and Clarinet

FIRST PREPARED ETUDE

SECOND PREPARED ETUDE

SIGHT-READING ETUDE

Fifth-Year
Flute

FIRST PREPARED ETUDE

SECOND PREPARED ETUDE

SIGHT-READING ETUDE

Fifth-Year
Saxophone

FIRST PREPARED ETUDE

SECOND PREPARED ETUDE

SIGHT-READING ETUDE

Fifth-Year
Trombone

FIRST PREPARED ETUDE

SECOND PREPARED ETUDE

SIGHT-READING ETUDE

Notes

Edwin Gordon is professor of music and education and Director of Music Education at the State University of New York at Buffalo.

1 The first-year results of this study are published in the *Journal of Research in Music Education* 18 no. 3 (1970), pp. 195–213; the second-year results in *Studies in the Psychology of Music*, Vol. 7 (1971), pp. 54–72; and the third-year results in *Studies in the Psychology of Music*, Vol. 8 (1972), pp. 45–64. The fourth-year, along with the fifth-year, results are reported in this paper.

2 These four schools were technically classified as culturally-disadvantaged under the provisions of the Elementary and Secondary School Act of 1965, Title 1.

3 Although some of these teachers did not remain in the Des Moines school system throughout the course of the study, they were replaced by teachers who possess similar abilities and interests.

4 It is interesting to note that the longitudinal analysis of the criterion scores of only those students who completed all five years of the study yielded substantively the same trend of results as that found for the total number of students who remained in the study each year.

5 The 55th percentile was selected as the dividing point to provide for proportionality in the statistical design of the study with a minimal loss of students.

6 Although supplementary analyses of the first-year results were undertaken, they are not summarized in this report primarily because the majority of students in the culturally-disadvantaged schools who served as control subjects in these analyses left the school district and were not available to participate in the ensuing years of the study. Therefore, first-year and subsequent-year comparisons were obviated.

7 Although 85 students remained in the study through four years of instruction, the results of only 80 students were analyzed. The results for five students in the culturally heterogeneous high aptitude group were randomly eliminated in the analyses in order to provide for proportionality in the statistical design.

8 Although 65 students remained in the study through five years of instruction, the results of only 63 students were analyzed. The results for two students in the culturally-heterogeneous high aptitude group were randomly eliminated in the analyses in order to provide for proportionality in the statistical design.

BIBLIOGRAPHY

Gordon, Edwin. *Musical Aptitude Profile*. Boston: Houghton Mifflin, 1965.

———. "A Comparison of the Performance of Culturally Disadvantaged Students with that of Culturally Heterogeneous Students on the Musical Aptitude Profile." *Psychology in the Schools* 15 (1967):260–268.

———. *A Three-Year Longitudinal Predictive Study of the Musical Aptitude Profile.* Studies in the Psychology of Music, vol. 5. Iowa City: University of Iowa Press, 1967.

———. "Taking into Account Musical Aptitude Differences Among Beginning Instrumental Students." *American Educational Research Journal* 15 (1970):41–53.

———. "The First-Year Results of a Five-Year Longitudinal Study of the Musical Achievement of Culturally Disadvantaged Students." *Journal of Research in Music Education* 18 (1970):195–213.

———. "The Second-Year Results of a Five-Year Longitudinal Study of the Musical Achievement of Culturally-Disadvantaged Students." *Experimental Research in the Psychology of Music: 7*. Studies in the Psychology of Music, vol. 7. Iowa City: University of Iowa Press, 1971.

———. "The Third-Year Results of a Five-Year Longitudinal Study of the Musical Achievement of Culturally-Disadvantaged Students." *Experimental Research in the Psychology of Music: 8*. Studies in the Psychology of Music, vol. 8. Iowa City: University of Iowa Press, 1972.

———— *Iowa Tests of Music Literacy*. Iowa City: Bureau of Educational Research and Service, University of Iowa, 1971.

Hill, John. "A Study of the Musical Achievement of Culturally Deprived Children and Culturally Advantaged Children at the Elementary School Level." *Experimental Research in the Psychology of Music*. Studies in the Psychology of Music, vol. 6. Iowa City: University of Iowa Press, 1970.

THE EFFECTS OF TONAL PATTERN TRAINING ON THE PERFORMANCE ACHIEVEMENT OF BEGINNING WIND INSTRUMENTALISTS[1]

Carol B. MacKnight

THEORETICAL BACKGROUND

One of the problems facing instrumental instruction today is the validity of the subject matter and procedures employed in the name of developing musical insights. Control over the instrument and mastery of notational symbols are often substituted for an understanding of music. Reasons for learning to read music are obscured. A plea for a more rational approach to music reading instruction is made in the belief that much of our effectiveness is mechanically based.[2]

> ... The end goal for a schoolboy playing the cornet is not the ability to push down the proper valves at the appropriate time, accompanied by measured lung power and calculated lip vibration. His ability to perform these tasks with exquisite skill cannot provide him with adequate insight into music, this ability ensures only that he is capable of the most elemental kind of stimulus-response maneuvering, a level not far above the performance of the Pavlovian dog.

The complexities of reading music are accentuated by the fact that the reader must simultaneously translate and reproduce notational symbols involving pitch, time, and expression. These symbols must be related to each other and to the sequences and phrases in which they occur, and finally to the over-all structure of the musical composition. The reader accomplishes this act from a relatively small perceptual span of three to five notes.[3] Reading music is thus a process which involves elements of perception, mediation, and conceptualization of musical patterns. This may be illustrated, as in Figure 1, by each element forming one of the points or corners of a triangle. Given a musical stimulus, each corner must ask questions from the other corners. The direction of questioning depends upon the musical development of the individual.

Perception is the first point of musical learning. Musical perception does not happen as a result of playing a musical instrument.[4] The auditory perception of musical sounds and the visual perception of musical symbols must be carefully taught.

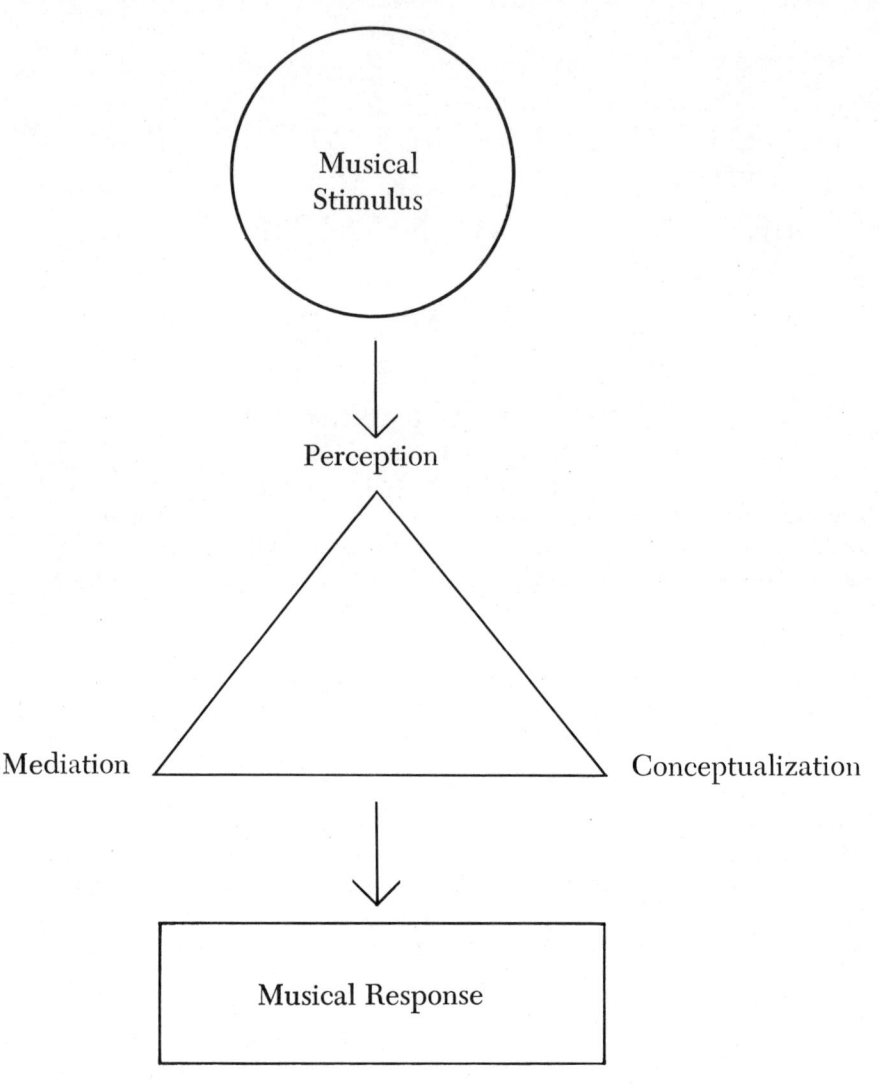

Figure 1. The Process of Reading Music

Aural understanding, which is the reflection of accurate auditory perception, results from intelligent thought and not from mechanical imitation, from judgments made independently by the child in terms of his understanding of basic musical concepts and not from judgments made for the child by the teacher.[5]

Mediation is the point at which the learner is able to organize previous auditory and visual perceptions into meaningful concepts. In musical learning conceptualization provides us with a basis for communicating musical ideas.

From our various perceptions of music, we develop the musical concepts that permit us to make comparisons and discriminations, to organize sound, to generalize and finally to apply emerging concepts to new musical situations.[6]

Conceptualization is the point of the music reading triangle most neglected in instrumental training.

From the above discussion, it is clear that music reading instruction which limits the meaning of pitch to that of letter names, fingerings, and lastly sounds is fundamentally and musically inadequate. First, a factor governing speed of comprehension is expectation. "The more unexpected the stimulus, the more questions the brain must ask to determine its identity."[7] Associating a mechanical response with the visual symbol reduces the reader's span of vision. Reading becomes a note-by-note process. When attention is so absorbed in the application of fingerings to written symbols, mental imagery is often impossible, limiting comprehension to an attempt to "get the notes right."

Second, relating each tone to the previous tone played in terms of highness or lowness is not to progress beyond basic perception to conceptualization. An appreciation of the tendency of tones and their desire for completion creates a system of expectation in the individual which makes possible the anticipation of tonal and rhythm patterns. Knowledge of tonal relationships enables the reader to recognize motives and their treatment as sequences, imitations, inversions, transpositions — to read with musical rather than mechanical understanding. Finally, it is the music, not the instrument that must ultimately tell the reader what to do.

Effective melodic reading requires that the reader apprehend a sequence of tones as a totality rather than as a number of separate tones. It is a sense of tonality that makes comprehensible a sequence of single tones as a unity.[8] The chief characteristic of tonality is that "within its conditions the role of any tone or group of tones does not reside in its direct sound quality but in its tonal relation to other tones or groups as well as in its relation to the entire pattern of a composition."[9] The importance of tonality in musical learning has been explored by Gordon,[10] De Yarman,[11] and Dittemore.[12] They concurred that students' understanding of music was dependent on their perception and conceptualization of tonality.

A frequent approach to a study of tonality is through learning a series of tonal patterns. Many researchers have investigated the effects of learning tonal patterns on ability to vocally read music. Petzold[13] reported that neither sex nor years of instrumental training were a factor in music reading competence. Klemish[14] discovered that exposure to a form of pseudo-notation prior to reading conventional notation was not a particularly useful technique in teaching young children to read music. She established, however, that six-year-olds could successfully learn a series of tonal patterns. In a later study Richardson[15] found that order of tonal pattern presentation did not affect the children's ability to learn a series of tonal patterns. Her results corroborate the findings of Jeffies[16] and Buttram.[17] Both investigators found no basis for sequencing a presentation of melodic intervals. In spite of that, Buttram discovered that harmonic intervals were most efficiently identified when a tonal center was first established. Furthermore, Marquis[18] considered the ability to perceive the basic quality of intervals in melodic sight-singing to be less important than the ability to perceive scalar, harmonic, and tonal changes across or surrounding intervals.

Few experimental studies have been designed to measure the effects of a particular treatment on the sight-reading skills of beginning wind instrumentalists. Of those reported, the studies which dealt with teaching procedures and reading material are of interest to this investigation. Noble[19] found the use of concept training to be a useful technique in developing elementary band sight-reading skill. Adaptations of certain Suzuki concepts were successfully employed by Sperti[20] with beginning clarinetists. Robison[21] effectively used a compositional approach with beginning wind instrumentalists. It is interesting to note that all the above approaches required some type of aural experience to clarify the meaning of notation.

With regard to music reading material, Williams[22] identified a learning sequence for beginning clarinetists based on junior high school band literature. Lacey[23] designed a trumpet method which was organized at a slower pace than existing methods. Nevertheless, the pace of the material made little difference to the development of sight-reading skills of beginning trumpeters. On the other hand, Froseth[24] found the combination of individualized group teaching techniques and special materials to be an efficient means of increasing the level of achievement of beginning instrumental students.

It would appear from the evidence presented that to be effective, instruction in music reading must consider the process involved in reading and the role of tonality in the developmental understanding of music. However, there is no experimental evidence that an effective procedure for teaching reading to beginning players consists of instruction which emphasizes tonality by utilizing the Tonic Sol-fa system to define a series of tonal patterns. It is to fill this gap in research that the present experimental study was undertaken.

PROBLEMS OF THE STUDY

The major problem under consideration was whether students who are taught a series of tonal patterns as single units attain a significantly higher level of musical achievement than students who are trained in note identification skill using traditional materials. Specific questions to be answered were:

1. Is there any difference between the scores of the experimental and control groups on the *Watkins-Farnum Performance Scale*[25] (WFPS)? Related to this question were:
   (a) Is the experimental treatment more effective than the control treatment for either brass or woodwind instruments?
   (b) Is the experimental treatment more effective than the control treatment for students of either high or low musical aptitude?

2. Is there any difference between the scores of the experimental and control groups on the *Music Achievement Test*[26] (MAT)? Related to this question were:
   (a) Is the experimental treatment more effective than the control treatment for either brass or woodwind instruments?
   (b) Is the experimental treatment more effective than the control treatment for students of either high or low musical aptitude?

3. Is there any difference between the scores of the experimental and the control groups on the pretest and posttest administration of the Student Attitude Questionnaire (SAQ)?

The desired outcome of the study was the identification of the more effective method of teaching reading to beginning instrumentalists so that this procedure could be incorporated into the elementary instrumental program in the Bay Shore Schools. Appendix A contains a definition of terms necessary for a better understanding of the study.

METHODOLOGY

The subjects for this study were approximately 90 fourth-graders enrolled in three of the four elementary schools in Bay Shore, N.Y., during the 1970–71 school year. The fourth school was not included on the basis that its band program was to be temporarily discontinued, a factor which could affect interest at some point during the project. By random selection, one school conducted the experimental program and the other two schools served as controls.

The students voluntarily elected to participate in the beginning instrumental program and chose the instruments they wished to play. Instruments selected included trumpets, cornets, horns, baritones, trombones, flutes, clarinets, and alto saxophones. Students were subsequently administered the *Musical Aptitude Profile*[27] (*MAP*) and a Student Attitude Questionnaire. Recent scores on the Lorge-Thorndike Intelligence Test were obtained from school records. Students' scores on the *Musical Aptitude Profile* and the Lorge-Thorndike Intelligence Test were used to statistically equate the experimental and control groups with respect to musical aptitude and intelligence — two variables which are relevant to music achievement.[28]

The students were given an initial trial on the instrument for six weeks. Following this period, those students judged incapable of making satisfactory progress in learning to read music because of continued difficulties in producing an adequate sound on the instrument were eliminated from the study. The observed difficulties appeared to be a total inability to coordinate the breath and tongue in the production of sound and the physical problems incurred by the addition of dental corrective measures. In that this investigation was concerned with measuring music reading achievement after a limited period of instruction, it was felt that unusual conditions such as these might have an affect on the outcome of the study. The total sample was reduced to 85 students who came from predominately middle-class homes. Appendix B lists the instrumentation of each group for those who began instruction in September and who were present to take the criterion tests in June.

Five certified New York state instrumental teachers expressed a strong interest in participating in the study. Three were selected to provide instruction based on the equivalency of their ratings using the following criteria:

1. Difficulty of music chosen to be performed at the conclusion of one year of lessons.

The minimum level for acceptance was performance in two keys, a range of a ninth, tempos of fast and slow, meters of $\frac{4}{4}$, $\frac{3}{4}$, and $\frac{2}{4}$, rhythm patterns of the difficulty of a dotted quarter and an eighth note, dynamics of loud and soft, and special signs including repeat signs and accidentals such as a sharp, flat, and natural.

2. Number of students who discontinued lessons during the first year of instruction.

The teachers chosen to participate in the study had a student dropout record no greater than 10 per cent.

3. Scores obtained on the *Minnesota Teacher Attitude Inventory*[29] (*MTAI*).

Teacher competence in the subject matter and in ability to create the kind of atmosphere where children can both learn and enjoy the learning process was an important factor to be considered. The *MTAI* is designed to measure teacher-pupil rapport. Other predictive uses of the *MTAI* were investigated by Standlee and Popham.[30] They found that it could also be used as a measure of over-all teaching effectiveness. Exploring this issue further, Popham and Trimble[31] tested the hypothesis that the *MTAI* discriminates between public school teachers judged to be "superior" and "inferior" in terms of general competence. They concluded that the *MTAI* measures not only the social atmosphere a teacher will maintain in the classroom, but also serves as an indication of a teacher's general competence. The three teachers selected scored higher than 90 per cent of the reference group, nonacademics with five years training. Their scores placed them in the "superior" teacher category.

One teacher elected to teach the experimental group. The other teachers were assigned to schools with regard to their other teaching assignments. Instruction consisted of one 30 minute homogeneous lesson each week for 32 weeks. Class size was limited to six students. Both the experimental and control groups covered the same pitches, rhythms, meters, keys, tempos, dynamics and special signs. The only variation in treatment was in the method and order of introducing pitch. The experimental group learned each new pitch as a member of a tonal pattern. The tonal patterns learned were: SO MI, SO MI DO, SO LA SO, MI RE DO, SO DO, SO FA MI, SO FA MI RE DO, DO LA SO, DO TI DO, and SO LA TI DO. Each pattern was taught as a single unit in three stages: (a) an aural presentation, (b) an aural-visual presentation, and (c) an aural-visual presentation of the pattern within a musical phrase. At each stage the teacher dictated the tonal pattern or phrase for the student to repeat (see Appendix C). The instructional book used by the experimental group was specially prepared with melodies containing the tonal patterns in order of presentation.[32]

Rhythm was presented to the experimental group phrase-wise. The students always responded to either the aural or visual presentation of melodic rhythm by chanting the phrase using the syllables "TA" for a ♩, "TI TI" for the ♫, and "TA-I TI" for the ♩ ♪. Durational values were taught by calling attention to the number of subtle pulses given to a particular rhythm syllable. Ability to read melodic rhythm notation by sensing phrase rhythm was the emphasis of the training.

The control group used a standard method book, *Breeze Easy*,[33] and proceeded in the manner dictated by the book. There, a new pitch may be found with its letter name and fingering at the top of the page. The new pitch must be learned in order to play one of the melodies on the same page. No effort is made to demonstrate the significance of the new pitch beyond that of a letter name, fingering, and sound.

Rhythm is taught as it numerically relates to a beat in this book. For example, a ♩ is taught as a quarter note having the durational value of one beat in ¼ meter. Melodic rhythm is practiced by counting, using a number to identify the ♩, "1 and" for ♫, and "1, 2 and" for the ♩ ♪. Unlike traditional instruction, the control group used rhythm syllables and were encouraged to sing assigned melodies with letter names or on a neutral syllable. Pitch distances were indicated by a flat hand signal. For a comparison of the procedures used by both groups see Appendix D.

During the final two weeks of the experiment, the investigator administered the *WFPS*, Form A, the *MAT*, Test 2, and a SAQ. Errors of performance on the *WFPS* include pitch, time, change of time, expression, slurs, rests, holds, pauses, and repeats. The author claims a reliability coefficient of .93 for all tests for musically select fourth grade groups and construct validity coefficients ranging from .64 to .94 with a median of .79 for performance groups. The *MAT* test consists of major-minor mode discrimination of chord and phrases; feeling for tonal center within cadences and phrases; and auditory-visual discrimination of pitch and rhythm. Test 2 has a reliability of .91 as estimated by the Kuder-Richardson 21 and a criterion-related validity coefficient of .92 based on the correlations between test scores and teachers' ratings of high and low achievers. The SAQ, based on semantic differential format, is a technique for observing and measuring the psychological meaning of concepts. Favorable attitudes toward the following concepts resulted in a high score: musical instrument, music book, music lesson, band teacher, singing, writing music, listening to music, reading music, practicing, and playing a solo. The test-retest reliability for the instrument was r = .81 (see Appendix E).

To answer the questions investigated in this study, the criterion scores were analysed for the main effects of treatment and the interaction between treatment and levels. For the purpose of data analyses, students were classified by treatment group, experimental or control; instrument, brass or woodwind; and musical aptitude, high, a percentile rank of greater than 50, or low, a percentile rank of less than 50 based on the national median for fourth grade students provided in the *MAP* Manual. Initially the analyses reported in the next section were carried out using a two-factor analysis of covariance with intelligence and musical aptitude scores as covariates. Both groups, however, were almost equivalent with respect to intelligence and musical aptitude scores.[34] It was therefore not unusual that analysis of variance on the test scores resulted in similar findings to those of analysis of covariance. For this reason, analysis of variance, a somewhat better known statistical technique, was used in the data analyses reported in this study.

SUMMARY OF RESULTS

Posttest means and standard deviations by treatment, instrument, and musical aptitude for the two groups on the *WFPS* are listed in Table 1.

To test the difference between the experimental conditions, tonal pattern instruction, and the control treatment, note identification instruction, analysis of variance using a three-factor least-squares design with unequal cells was employed.[35] A summary of the results of the analysis is presented in Table 2.

It can be observed that the main effect of treatment was statistically significant ($F = 18.76$, $p < .05$). An examination of Table 1 readily indicates that the experimental students achieved a higher level of sight-reading skill

Table 1

Means and Standard Deviations for Scores on the Watkins-Farnum Performance Scale

Level	Experimental Group			Control Group		
	N	M	S.D.	N	M	S.D.
Treatment	39	38.73	12.69	35	25.95	13.62
Brass Instruments	17	39.31	13.23	16	26.76	14.28
Woodwind Instruments	22	38.16	11.12	19	25.15	11.42
High Musical Aptitude	28	41.32	10.74	27	35.68	10.76
Low Musical Aptitude	11	36.15	11.69	8	16.23	11.66

Table 2

Summary of Analysis of Variance of Results on the Watkins-Farnum Performance Scale

Source of Variance	df	MS	F Ratio
Treatment (T)	1	2169.25	18.76*
Instrument (I)	1	21.89	<1
Musical Aptitude (MA)	1	1724.79	14.91*
T X I	1	0.92	<1
T X MA	1	672.11	5.81*
I X MA	1	374.68	3.24
Error	67	115.65	

*Significant at the 5% level.

(M = 38.73) than the control students (M = 25.95). Neither the effect of instrument (F = < 1, p > .05) nor the interaction of treatment and instrument (F = < 1, p > .05) was significant. Thus, there is no evidence that tonal pattern instruction was more beneficial to either brass students or woodwind students. However, the effect of musical aptitude (F = 14.91, p < .05) and the interaction of treatment and musical aptitude (F = 5.81, p < .05) were found to be significant. Table 1 reveals the greater difference between levels of musical aptitude occurred among control students. The posttest mean score of 36.15 for low musical aptitude students who received the tonal pattern treatment was significantly higher than the mean of 16.23 for low musical aptitude control students (F = 11.74, p < .05), based on a simple-effects analysis. The five point mean difference between the high musical aptitude experimental and control students was not significant (F = 3.93, p > .05). No other interactions were significant.

The posttest means and standard deviations for the *MAT* total scores for both groups are given in Table 3. The statistical analysis of the data appears in Table 4.

Table 3

Means and Standard Deviations for Scores on the
Music Achievement Test

Level	Experimental Group			Control Group		
	N	M	S.D	N	M	S.D.
Treatment	39	33.60	9.56	35	28.35	10.30
Brass Instruments	17	32.38	9.97	16	26.54	10.76
Woodwind Instruments	22	34.81	8.40	19	30.15	8.63
High Musical Aptitude	28	41.11	8.09	27	29.22	8.11
Low Musical Aptitude	11	26.08	8.80	8	27.48	8.80

Table 4

Summary of Analysis of Variance of Results on the
Music Achievement Test

Source of Variance	df	MS	F Ratio
Treatment (T)	1	366.19	5.58*
Instrument (I)	1	105.22	1.60
Musical Aptitude (MA)	1	789.89	12.17*
T X I	1	5.99	<1
T X MA	1	581.58	8.86*
I X MA	1	183.47	2.79
Error	67	65.67	

*Significant at the 5% level.

This analysis yielded a statistically significant difference ($F = 5.58$, $p < .05$) between the mean score of 33.60 attained by the experimental group and the mean control score of 28.35. The effect of instrument ($F = 1.60$, $p > .05$) and the interaction of treatment and instrument ($F = < 1$, $p > .05$) were not found to be significant. However, the main effect of musical aptitude ($F = 12.17$, $p < .05$) and the interaction of treatment and musical aptitude ($F = 8.86$, $p < .05$) were both significant. No other interactions approached significance.

An inspection of Table 3 suggests that the two treatments were differentially effective with high and low musical aptitude students. As indicated in this table high musical aptitude students who received the experimental treatment scored 12 points higher than control trained students of similar aptitude, but experimental students classified as low musical aptitude students scored one point lower than their control trained counterparts. The 12 point difference between high musical aptitude groups on the posttest was statistically significant ($F = 29.77$, $p < .05$). This implies that tonal pattern instruction was quite effective with students of high musical aptitude, whereas with students of low musical aptitude it had less effect in developing auditory-visual discrimination.

It is interesting to note that the *MAT* achievement scores of low musical aptitude students under the experimental treatment contrasts sharply with their performance on the *WFPS*. Experimental students of low musical aptitude made considerable progress in learning to sight read music as measured by the *WFPS*. Failure to detect a similar effect suggests that the low musical aptitude students have reached a plateau in their ability to match an aural stimulus with a visual symbol as required on the *MAT* test.

Other alternative points of view may be offered to explain this rather provocative finding. First, it may be too early for the experimental effect to develop with students of low musical aptitude. Second, if more positive results in auditory visual discrimination are to be anticipated at the conclusion of the first year of instrumental lessons, then the instruction in music reading as employed in this study provided insufficient training in listening and following a melodic sequence from left to right. An examination of the data indicates that low musical aptitude students achieved a higher level of performance on the first part of the *MAT* test where they were required to attend to the auditory presentation of information alone, but that they were less able to attend to the simultaneous presentation of auditory-visual information. It is conceivable then that low musical aptitude students took longer to integrate their bimodal responses and that additional training in left to right scanning at different tempos might improve their performance. Third, research has found that age is directly related to competence in the auditory perception of the melodic elements of music.[36] Therefore, it is possible that by the age of ten the period for developing aural skills to any appreciable extent may have passed for students of low musical aptitude. Finally, the *MAT* was administered during the final hours of the school day. Low musical aptitude students may not have been as attentive on a test requiring a written response as they were on the *WFPS* where greater personal involvement was necessary in order to respond instrumentally.

The results of the attitude study of students in both treatment groups before and after instruction are reported in Tables 6 and 7.

From these tables it is clear that there were only slight differences between the pretest and posttest results for each group and between groups on the 10 concepts. Consequently, no further analysis was performed on the data. A

Table 5

Means and Standard Deviations for All Concepts on the
Pretest Administration of the Student
Attitude Questionnaire

Concept	Experiment Group N = 43		Control Group N = 42	
	M	S.D	M	S.D.
1. Musical Instrument	10.15	4.07	9.24	4.49
2. Music Book	8.65	5.07	8.96	4.39
3. Music Lesson	9.95	4.81	9.64	3.94
4. Band Teacher	10.60	4.06	10.58	3.25
5. Singing	4.55	8.08	5.98	6.85
6. Writing Music	6.30	6.26	5.87	7.27
7. Listening to Music	9.40	5.23	8.93	4.85
8. Reading Music	8.33	6.48	8.04	5.32
9. Practicing	8.83	5.97	8.89	4.37
10. Playing a Solo	7.25	6.38	7.40	5.89
All Concepts	84.00	39.91	83.53	32.63

Table 6

Means and Standard Deviations for All Concepts on the
Posttest Administration of the Student
Attitude Questionnaire

Concept	Experimental Group N = 35		Control Group N = 32	
	M	S.D.	M	S.D.
1. Musical Instrument	10.97	3.28	11.72	2.80
2. Music Book	9.71	4.56	10.25	5.59
3. Music Lesson	11.43	2.76	11.44	3.32
4. Band Teacher	12.86	1.83	12.63	1.93
5. Singing	6.40	8.47	5.31	9.60
6. Writing Music	8.11	6.18	7.97	7.42
7. Listening to Music	10.06	3.61	10.91	5.36
8. Reading Music	10.26	3.36	10.94	4.18
9. Practicing	10.31	4.36	10.88	3.81
10. Playing a Solo	8.91	5.96	11.75	4.20
All Concepts	99.03	32.61	101.30	28.71

reexamination of the data showed that the attitude scores of both groups were negatively skewed on the SAQ. Students tended to use many more positive evaluative qualifiers (Interesting, Pleasurable, etc.) than negative evaluative qualifiers (Boring, Painful, etc.). A highly positive effect was also noted in the data of those students who planned to terminate music lessons. Boucher and Osgood[37] reported a similar tendency. In explaining this result, they remark that, although positive evaluative words appear earlier than their negative opposites across the age levels from 7 through 11, children and adults alike tend to see and report the quality of something in positive terms. According to them, the reason for this optimism lies somewhere in our social structure and the circumstances required to maintain it. "It is hard," they say, "to imagine human groups whose members persistently look for and talk about the ugly things in life and in their neighbors long remaining together."[38] In addition to these factors, the stabilization of the connotative meaning of musical concepts, may be partially attributed to a good match between teacher behavior and characteristics of students. Research has shown that student attitudes toward the teacher and the learning activities appear to be related to teacher behavior.[39]

CONCLUSIONS

In reading music the beginner experiences different levels of perceiving, remembering, organizing, conceptualizing and anticipating tonal and rhythm patterns. Skill in reading music is dependent upon the perception and conceptualization of tonality. A sense of tonality gives meaning to musical sounds and the notational symbols they represent. It is essential to the recollection of patterns of tones, and thus fundamental for the understanding of music whose essence is relationships. The results of this research suggest that a study of tonality based on the recognition of a series of tonal patterns facilitates the musical achievement of beginning wind instrumentalists. Without this training, pitch considered more or less in isolation loses its meaning and becomes a mere label. The evidence shows that those students trained in note identification were less able than the tonal pattern trained students to relate auditory patterns to their corresponding patterns in print, a measure of auditory-visual discrimination (MAT), or reverse the process by responding to visual patterns with the appropriate sound sequences, an indication of instrumental sight-reading ability ($WFPS$).

The nonsignificant treatment by instrument interaction provides evidence that the effect of treatment was independent of instrument, that is, approximately the same difference between the experimental and control groups was found regardless of the levels of instrument. However, on both the $WFPS$ and the MAT a significant treatment by musical interaction was found. This means that the difference between the experimental and control treatments was not independent of levels of musical aptitude. The data suggest that the low musical aptitude students sight read on their instruments better under the tonal pattern approach. For students of high musical aptitude either treatment proved to be effective. The achievement of low musical aptitude students on the *MAT* was approximately the same for either treatment condition. Nevertheless, high musical aptitude students profited from learning a series of tonal patterns as indicated by the fact that they achieved significantly higher scores than high musical aptitude students in the control group on the *MAT*.

The test of the main effect of treatments revealed statistically significant differences in favor of the experimental treatment on the *WFPS* and *MAT*. Thus, it was concluded that tonal pattern training results in greater average musical achievement than note identification training. The data strongly indicates that a high level of musical understanding as well as proficiency on the instrument can be achieved when instruction emphasizes: (a) identification of musical patterns, (b) active involvement in listening, (c) singing with tonal syllables, (d) chanting with rhythm syllables, (e) thought and conceptualization, and (f) preorganized reading materials which introduce tones and rhythms in their most frequent patterns.

Though the present results are encouraging, they are subject to cautious interpretation. The teaching procedures employed in this study were applied to a small sample from a single school population. The possibility remains that the significant differences found were in part a function of other variables, such as teacher effectiveness, and not method. The resultant generalizations are therefore limited to the particular sample used. Future studies are needed to determine whether or not similar results can be obtained over time and place with different student populations and teachers. Hopefully other investigators will be stimulated by the information secured within the limitations of this study to investigate an important problem in the area of instrumental music instruction.

APPENDIX A

Definition of Terms

The following are definitions of terms used in this study.

1. Music reading is the process of perceiving, translating, and reproducing instrumentally, at first sight, the various symbols of notation.
2. Tonal patterns are melodic configurations containing two to five tones and describing the tendency of scale tones.
3. Tonality refers to the tendency of tones. The tones in a melody are either active or inactive in nature. The most restful sounding tone is the tonic, or tonal center.
4. Specifics refer to fingerings and to the various notational symbols, such as clefs, key signatures, meter signatures, bars, accidentals, note values, letter names, and similar items.
5. Traditional instruction refers to the kind of instruction which stresses identification of notational symbols and the mechanics of playing the instrument.
6. Rhythmic syllables are represented by the words "TA" for a quarter note, "TI" for an eighth note, and "TA-I" for a dotted quarter note.
7. Mechanics of playing an instrument refers to the physical aspects of musical performance, such as embrochure position, body position, articulation, breathing, and fingering.
8. Hand signals are of two distinct types. Flat hand signals are used to indicate pitch distance. Hand postures, developed by John Curwen in 1870, represent a particular degree of the scale and the tendency of that scale degree, while also indicating pitch distance. The two types of hand signals are illustrated below.

Figure 2
HAND SIGNALS

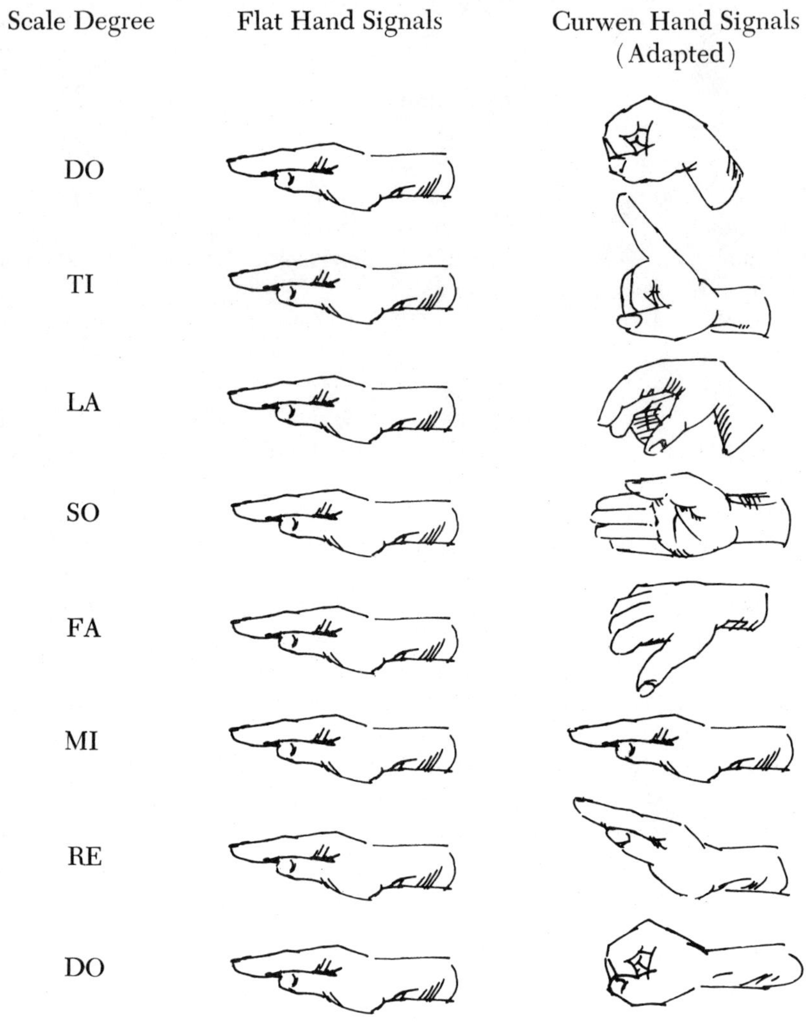

Scale Degree	Flat Hand Signals	Curwen Hand Signals (Adapted)
DO		
TI		
LA		
SO		
FA		
MI		
RE		
DO		

APPENDIX B

Instrumentation

	September		June	
	Experimental	Control	Experimental	Control
Trumpet/Cornet	10	8	9	7
Horn	4	2	4	1
Baritone	1	0	1	0
Trombone	5	7	5	6
Clarinet	15	11	13	10
Flute	7	10	7	8
Saxophone	1	4	0	3
	43	42	39	35

APPENDIX C

Procedure for Learning Tonal Patterns

Stage 1 (Aural)	Stage 2 (Aural-Visual)	Stage 3 (Aural-Visual)
Stimulus: Tonal Pattern (T.P.)	T.P.	T.P. Within a Phrase
Listen: T.P.	Listen and Read T.P.	Listen and Read Phrase
Repeat: Sing with Syllables and use Hand Signals (H.S.)	Sing with Syllables and use H.S.	Read and Chant Phrase
Listen: T.P.	Listen and Read T.P.	Listen and Read Phrase
Repeat: Sing with Letter Names (L.N.) and Finger the Instrument	Sing with L.N. and Finger the Instrument	Sing with Syllables and use H.S.
Listen: T.P.	Listen and Read T.P.	Listen and Read Phrase
Repeat: Play	Play	Sing with L.N. and Finger the Instrument
		Play

APPENDIX D

Methods of Teaching Music Reading

Elements		Experimental Group[a]	Control Group[b]
Melody:	Approach New Tonal Presentation	Tonal Patterns Aural approach within a tonal pattern Visual approach of an isolated tonal pattern Aural-visual approach of a tonal pattern within a melody	Individual Pitches Aural-visual approach of an isolated pitch Aural-visual approach of the pitch within a melody

	Activities	Singing:
		  Letter names
		  Tonal syllables
		The Curwen Hand Signals
			Singing:
			  Letter names
			  Neutral syllables
			Flat Hand Signal

Rhythm:	Approach Activities	Rhythm Patterns Chanting	Individual Notes Chanting Counting Clapping

[a] Hearing and Playing Musical Patterns
[b] *Breeze Easy*

APPENDIX E

Student Attitude Questionnaire

A Student Attitude Questionnaire was constructed based on a semantic differential format according to the criteria given by Osgood.[40] The semantic differential is a method of observing and measuring the psychological meaning of concepts. A concept refers, in this case, to the stimulus to which the subject responds in terms of degrees.

From a list of musical concepts, ten concepts were selected that were closely related to the student's musical experiences and expected to produce individual differences. They were: musical instrument, music book, music lesson, band teacher, singing, writing music, listening to music, reading music, practicing, and playing a solo. The instrument consisted of seven bipolar adjectives placed at opposite ends of a five-point scale, e.g.: Interesting — — — — — Boring. The adjectives included: Interesting-Boring; Painful-Pleasurable; Useful-Useless; Unimportant-Important; Successful-Unsuccessful; Bad-Good; Easy-Difficult. Only the evaluative factor was used.

The position of the negative ends of each scale was randomized. Values of $-2, -1, 0, +1, +2$ were assigned to the adjective positions on the interposed ordinal scale. Scales such as Interesting-Boring were flipped from minus to plus before scoring. The rating values of each concept represented a Part Score, and the sum of the Part Scores for the ten concepts represented a Total Score. More favorable attitudes or a higher score resulted when the position of a stimulus concept was rated on the scale closest to the following poles: Interesting, Pleasurable, Useful, Important, Successful, Good, and Easy.

The SAQ was administered twice at an interval of one week as a measure of test-retest reliability. The Pearson product-moment coefficients were obtained by correlating over the Total Scores. A single average score (Part Score) was assigned each concept as based on the mean scale position of that concept for all scales and all students. The Pearson product-moment coefficient for the Total Score on the test-retest administration was .81, representing a fairly high degree of reliability.

Notes

Carol B. MacKnight is educational consultant, Education School, University of Massachusetts, Amherst, Massachusetts.

1   This article is a summary of the author's Ed.D. thesis entitled *The Development and Evaluation of Tonal Pattern Instruction in Music Reading for Beginning Wind Instrumentalists* (University of Massachusetts, 1973).

2   *Comprehensive Musicianship: An Anthology of Evolving Thought* (Contemporary Music Project, Music Educators National Conference, 1971), p. 68.

3   H. E. Weaver, "Studies of Ocular Behavior in Music Reading," *Psychological Monographs* (1943), p. 3.

4   Bennett Reimer, "Performance and Aesthetic Sensitivity," *Music Educators Journal* 54 (1968): 108.

5   R. G. Petzold, "The Development of Auditory Perception of Musical Sounds by Children in the First Six Grades," *Journal of Research in Music Education* 11 (1963):43.

6   M. P. Zimmerman, "Percept and Concept: Implications of Piaget," *Music Educators Journal* 56 (1970): 49.

7   Rosamund Shuter, *The Psychology of Musical Ability* (London: Methuen, 1968), p. 201.

8   J. Jersild, *Ear Training* (Copenhagen: Wilhelm Hanse, 1956), p. 11.

9   Norman Cazden, "Tonal Function and Sonority in the Study of Harmony," *Journal of Research in Music Education* 12 (1964):22.

10   Kate Gordon, "Some Tests on the Memorizing of Musical Themes," *Journal of Experimental Psychology* 2 (1917):93–99.

11   Robert De Yarman, "An Experimental Analysis of the Development of Rhythmic and Tonal Capabilities of Kindergarten and First Grade Children" (Ph.D. diss., University of Iowa, 1971).

12   Edgar E. Dittemore, "An Investigation of Some Musical Capabilities of Elementary School Children," *Experimental Research in the Psychology of Music*, Studies in the Psychology of Music, Vol. 6 (Iowa City, Iowa: University of Iowa Press, 1970), pp. 1–44.

13   R. G. Petzold, "The Perception of Music Symbols in Music Reading by Normal Children and by Children Gifted Musically," *Journal of Experimental Education* 28 (1960):316–317.

14   J. J. Klemish, "A Comparative Study of Two Methods of Teaching Music Reading to First Grade" (Ph.D. diss., University of Wisconsin, 1968).

15   H. V. Richardson, "An Experimental Study Utilizing Two Procedures for Teaching Music Reading to Children in Second Grade" (Ph.D. diss., University of Wisconsin, 1971).

16   T. B. Jeffries, "The Effects of Order of Presentation and Knowledge of Results on the Aural Recognition of Melodic Intervals" (Ph.D. diss., University of California, 1965).

17   J. B. Buttram, "Perception of Musical Intervals," *Perceptual and Motor Skills* 28(1969):391–394.

18   J. H. Marquis, "A Study of Interval Problems in Sightsinging Performance with Consideration of the Effect of Context" (Ph.D. diss., University of Iowa, 1963).

19   R. F. Noble, "A Study of the Effects of a Concept Teaching Curriculum on Achievement in Performance in Elementary School Beginning Bands" (Washington, D.C.: Office of Education, Bureau of Research, 1969).

20   J. Sperti, "Adaptation of Certain Aspects of the Suzuki Method to the Teaching of the Clarinet: An Experimental Investigation Testing the Comparative Effectiveness of Two Different Pedagogical Methodologies" (Ed.D. diss., New York University, 1970).

21   W. H. Robison, "An Experiment to Determine the Effectiveness of Music Composition as an Aid to Musical Maturation in Fifth-grade Beginning Wind Instrument Students" (Ed.D. diss., University of Georgia, 1970).

22   R. E. Williams, "A Learning Sequence for Beginners on the Clarinet Based on an Investigation of Musical and Manipulative Difficulties Found in Junior High Band Music" (Ed.D. diss., University of Illinois, 1969).

23   R. M. Lacey, "The Teaching of Trumpet Using Special Material" (Ed.D. diss., Boston University, 1969).

24   J. O. Froseth, "An Investigation of the Use of Musical Aptitude Profile Scores in the Instruction of Beginning Students in Instrumental Music" (Ph.D. diss., University of Iowa, 1968).

25 J. G. Watkins and S. E. Farnum, *The Watkins-Farnum Performance Scale* (Winona, Minn.: Hal Leonard Music, 1954).
26 R. Colwell, *Music Achievement Test* (Chicago: Follett Educational Corporation, 1969).
27 Edwin Gordon, *Musical Aptitude Profile* (Boston: Houghton Mifflin, 1965).
28 W. T. Young, "An Investigation of the Relative and Combined Power of Musical Aptitude, General Intelligence, and Academic Achievement Tests to Predict Musical Attainment" (Ph.D. diss., University of Iowa, 1969).
29 W. W. Cook, C. H. Leeds, and R. Callis, *Minnesota Teacher Attitude Inventory Manual* (New York: The Psychological Corporation, 1951).
30 L. S. Standless and W. J. Popham, "The MTAI as a Predictor of Over-all Teacher Effectiveness," *Journal of Educational Research* 42 (1959):319–320.
31 W. J. Popham and R. R. Trimble, "The Minnesota Teacher Attitude Inventory as an Index of General Teaching Competence," *Educational and Psychological Measurement* 20 (1960):512.
32 C. B. MacKnight and J. E. Young, *Hearing and Playing Musical Patterns for Wind Instruments* (Elizabethtown, Pa.: Continental Press, forthcoming).
33 J. Kinyon, *Breeze Easy* (New York: Witmark, 1959).
34 Lorge-Thorndike Intelligence Test:
   Experimental Group   M = 114.81; S.D. = 10.35
   Control Group   M = 114.38; S.D. = 10.66
   Musical Aptitude Profile:
   Experimental Group   M = 46.11; S.D. = 5.76
   Control Group   M = 46.74; S.D. = 6.11
35 W. R. Harvey, "Instructions for Use of LSMLGP," mimeographed (Ohio State University, February, 1968).
36 Petzold, "Auditory Perception," p. 32.
37 J. Boucher and C. E. Osgood, "The Pollyanna Hypothesis," *Journal of Verbal Learning and Verbal Behavior* 8 (1969):7–8.
38 Boucher and Osgood, "Pollyanna Hypothesis," p. 8.
39 N. A. Flanders, B. M. Morrison, and E. L. Brode, "Changes in Pupil Attitudes During the School Year," *Journal of Educational Psychology* 50 (1968):338.
40 C. E. Osgood, G. J. Suci, and P. H. Tannenbaum, *The Measurement of Meaning* (Chicago: University of Illinois Press, 1957), chapters 3 and 4.

BIBLIOGRAPHY

Bean, Kenneth L. "An Experimental Approach to the Reading of Music." *Psychological Monographs* 50 (1938):1–80.

Boucher, J., and Osgood, C. E. "The Pollyanna Hypothesis," *Journal of Verbal Learning and Verbal Behavior* 8 (1969):1–8.

Buttram, J. B. "Perception of Musical Intervals." *Perceptual and Motor Skills* 28 (1969):391–394.

Cazden, Norman. "Tonal Function and Sonority in the Study of Harmony." *Journal of Research in Music Education* 12 (1964):21–34.

Colwell, Richard. *Music Achievement Test.* Chicago: Follett Educational Corp., 1969.

Comprehensive Musicianship: An Anthology of Evolving Thought. Contemporary Music Project, Music Educators National Conference, 1971.

Cook, W. W.; Leeds, C. H.; and Callis, R. *Minnesota Teacher Attitude Inventory Manual.* New York: Psychological Corp., 1951.

De Yarman, Robert. "An Experimental Analysis of the Development of Rhythmic and Tonal Capabilities of Kindergarten and First Grade Children." Ph.D. dissertation, University of Iowa, 1971.

Dittemore, Edgar. "An Investigation of Some Musical Capabilities of Elementary School Children." *Experimental Research in the Psychology of Music*, Studies in the Psychology of Music, vol. 6. Iowa City, University of Iowa Press, 1970.

Flanders, N. A.; Morrison, B. M.; and Brode, E. L. "Changes in Pupil Attitudes During the School Year." *Journal of Educational Psychology* 50 (1968):334–338.

Froseth, J. O. "An Investigation of the Use of Musical Aptitude Profile Scores in the Instruction of Beginning Students in Instrumental Music." Ph.D. dissertation, University of Iowa, 1968.

Gordon, Edwin. *Musical Aptitude Profile*. Boston: Houghton Mifflin, 1965.

———. *The Psychology of Music Teaching*. Englewood Cliffs: Prentice-Hall, 1971.

Gordon, Kate. "Some Tests on the Memorizing of Musical Themes." *Journal of Experimental Psychology* 2 (1917):93–99.

Harvey, W. R. "Instructions for Use of LSMLGP." Mimeographed. Columbus, Ohio: Ohio State University, 1968.

Jacobsen, O. I. "An Analytical Study of Eye-Movements in Reading Vocal and Instrumental Music." *Journal of Musicology* 3 (1942):223–226.

Jeffries, T. B. "The Effects of Order of Presentation and Knowledge of Results on the Aural Recognition of Melodic Intervals." Ph.D. dissertation, University of California, 1965.

Jersild, J. *Ear Training*. Copenhagen: Wilhelm Hansen, 1956.

King, H. A. "A Study of the Relationship of Music Reading and I.Q. Scores." *Journal of Research in Music Education* 12 (1964):35–37.

Kinyon, John. *Breeze Easy*. New York: Witmark, 1959.

Klemish, J. J. "A Comparative Study of Two Methods of Teaching Music Reading to First Grade." Ph.D. dissertation, University of Wisconsin, 1968.

Lacey, R. M. "The Teaching of Trumpet Using Special Material." Ed.D. dissertation, Boston University, 1969.

MacKnight, C. B., and Young, J. E. *Hearing and Playing Musical Patterns for Wind Instruments*. Elizabethtown, Pa.: Continental Press, 1974.

Marquis, J. H. "A Study of Interval Problems in Sightseeing Performance with Consideration of the Effect of Context." Ph.D. dissertation, University of Iowa, 1963.

Murphy, H. A. *Teaching Musicianship*. New York: Coleman-Ross, 1950.

Mursell, J. L. *Music Education Principles and Programs*. New York: Silver Burdett, 1956.

Mursell, J. L., and Glenn, M. *The Psychology of School Music Teaching*. New York: Silver Burdett, 1931.

Noble, R. F. "A Study of the Effects of a Concept Teaching Curriculum on Achievement in Performance in Elementary School Beginning Bands." Washington, D.C.: Office of Education, Bureau of Research, 1969.

Ortmann, Otto. "Span of Vision in Note Reading." In *Yearbook of the Music Educators National Conference*. Washington, D.C.: Music Educators National Conference, 1937.

Osgood, C. E.; Suci, G. J.; and Tannenbaum, P. H. *The Measurement of Meaning*. Chicago: University of Illinois Press, 1957.

Petzold, R. G. "The Perception of Music Symbols in Music Reading by Normal Children and by Children Gifted Musically." *Journal of Experimental Education* 28 (1960):271–319.

──. "The Development of Auditory Perception of Musical Sounds by Children in the First Six Grades." *Journal of Research in Music Education* 11 (1963):21–43.

Popham, W. J. and Trimble, R. R. "The Minnesota Teacher Attitude Inventory as an Index of General Teaching Competence." *Educational and Psychological Measurement* 20 (1960):509–512.

Reimer, Bennett. "Performance and Aesthetic Sensitivity." *Music Educators Journal* 54 (1968):27–114.

Richardson, H. V. "An Experimental Study Utilizing Two Procedures for Teaching Music Reading to Children in Second Grade." Ph.D. dissertation, University of Wisconsin, 1971.

Robison, W. H. "An Experiment to Determine the Effectiveness of Music Composition as an Aid to Musical Maturation in Fifth-grade Beginning Wind Instrument Students." Ed.D. dissertation, University of Georgia, 1970.

Sessions, Roger. *The Musical Experience of Composer, Performer, Listener.* New York: Atheneum, 1966.

Shuter, Rosamund. *The Psychology of Musical Ability.* London: Methuen, 1968.

Sperti, John. "Adaptation of Certain Aspects of the Suzuki Method to the Teaching of the Clarinet: An Experimental Investigation Testing the Comparative Effectiveness of Two Different Pedagogical Methodologies." Ed.D. dissertation, New York University, 1970.

Standlee, L. S., and Popham, W. J. "The MTAI as a Predictor of Over-all Teacher Effectiveness." *Journal of Educational Research* 42 (1959):319–320.

Watkins, J. G., and Farnum, S. E. *The Watkins-Farnum Performance Scale.* Winona, Minn.: Hal Leonard Music, 1954.

Weaver, H. E. "Studies of Ocular Behavior in Music Reading." *Psychological Monographs* 55 (1943):1–30.

Williams, R. E. "A Learning Sequence for Beginners on the Clarinet Based on an Investigation of Musical and Manipulative Difficulties Found in Junior High Band Music." Ed.D. dissertation, University of Illinois, 1969.

Winer, B. J. *Statistical Principles in Experimental Design.* New York: McGraw Hill, 1962.

Young, W. T. "An Investigation of the Relative and Combined Power of Musical Aptitude, General Intelligence, and Academic Achievement Test to Predict Musical Attainment." Ph.D. dissertation, University of Iowa, 1969.

Zimmerman, M. P. "Percept and Concept: Implications of Piaget." *Music Educators Journal* 56 (1970):49–54.

AN EXPERIMENTAL ANALYSIS OF THE DEVELOPMENT OF TONAL CAPABILITIES OF FIRST GRADE CHILDREN

Philip H. Miller

In *The Study of Music in the Elementary School: A Conceptual Approach*,[1] it is stated that various types of tonal concepts should constitute elementary general music curriculums. In "Concepts about Melody," it is suggested that, in general, children should be exposed to music written in usual modes[2] and unusual modes[3] and to nontonal music.[4] Therefore, it would seem that the music educator's role, in part, is to teach children to understand broad aspects of tonal characteristics of music.

The appropriate sequence of presenting tonal concepts to children is probably as important as the nature of the content of tonal concepts in elementary music curriculums. However, little objective evidence is available regarding the grade level, age, or stage of musical development at which children might most appropriately receive instruction in singing nontonal songs and songs in usual and unusual modes. House states that although concept development is cyclical, ". . . the experiences *themselves* do occur in a natural sequence which can establish an effective working pattern."[5] It is unfortunate that no sequence for the provision of such musical experiences is offered by House. Meyer also stresses the importance of early musical experiences but neither is he specific about the types of sequence of experiences that should be offered.

> The habits and dispositions which facilitate (musical) perception and make communication possible are acquired not with one, two, or perhaps even a hundred encounters with a particular (musical) style, or style-class but become part of our very being through countless experiences that begin in infancy.
>
> Because our most firmly rooted habits of thought and discrimination are learned in infancy and early childhood, the musical style system we first experience is the one that tends to dominate our perception and cognition of music throughout our lives.[6]

In that basic music series reflect current philosophy in music education, it is interesting to observe the musical content and sequence which they comprise. The tonal content of songs found in kindergarten and first grade music books is limited primarily to songs in the major mode.

It is interesting to speculate just why there is such a paucity of songs in the music series in the minor and unusual modes and practically no nontonal songs. Regarding sequence in the presentation of tonal concepts, it is possible that music educators support the notion that children should first learn to perform songs in the major mode before they learn to perform songs in the minor and unusual modes, and nontonal songs. Or, it may be that music educators assume that songs in the minor and unusual modes and nontonal songs are too difficult for young children to learn. However, the following statements by Meyer and Pfeiffer, respectively, challenge both of these assumptions.

> The human mind is capable of maintaining many different and even contradictory behavior systems simultaneously and of bringing these into play at appropriate times.[7]

> Between two and six the cortex completes the major part of its growth, a fact that jibes nicely with theories concerning the importance of early childhood experiences.[8]

Meyer continues:

> . . . insofar as serial music is preceptually highly complex and irregular, it is difficult for children, and perhaps even adults, to bring relevant sensor-motor behavior into play. On the other hand, since it is also clear that the human mind is capable of astonishing feats of learning, the point at which complexity and irregularity inhibit or thwart learning must be left open.[9]

> It is important to remember that early learning is critical, not merely because it is *first*, but because in childhood the connections and pathways of the nervous system are still largely unspecified.[10]

Although music psychologists tend to believe that young children should learn to understand broad aspects of tonality in music, they provide only little insight into how or when children best develop these understandings. For example, Mursell explains:

> Musical growth turns upon a progressive and continuously developing realization of what music actually is. Therefore at least a dawning realization should come from the earliest years.[11]

The need for objective information which is pertinent to appropriate sequential instructional procedures through experimental research becomes clearly evident when Mursell continues:

> In introducing significant musical concepts, there is not any need to wait for a supposititious moment when children will be "ready" to deal with them. They can occur in immature form very early indeed. For instance, it has been claimed that

the teaching of the minor tonality should come quite late in the sequence. But an authentic feeling for the difference between major and minor can be established almost from the beginning. . . . Instead of teaching the minor tonality at some one predetermined point, it is, so to speak, spread out through a number of years. So also with all other musical concepts.[12]

De Yarman extensively investigated young children's performance and understanding of rhythmic concepts in his study, *An Experimental Analysis of the Development of Rhythmic and Tonal Capabilities of Kindergarten and First Grade Children.*[13] However, an aspect of this study did bear on the tonal capabilities of young children. Regarding tonal understanding, De Yarman found that children who receive regular instruction, as outlined in the Iowa City Community School District's *Music Curriculum Guide,*[14] in tonal and nontonal music perform songs in major and minor tonalities better than their peers who receive regular instruction in only tonal music. These results seem to indicate that exposure to broad aspects of melodic characteristics of music reinforces children's performance and understanding of the more familiar tonal music.

Problems of the Study

The specific questions that were considered in the present study were as follows:
1. Do children who receive regular instruction in learning to sing songs in usual modes perform usual mode songs better than children who receive regular instruction in learning to sing songs in unusual modes and/or nontonal songs in addition to songs in usual modes?
2. Do children who receive regular instruction in learning to sing songs in usual and unusual modes perform usual and unusual mode songs better than children who receive regular instruction in learning to sing nontonal songs in addition to songs in usual and unusual modes?
3. Do children who receive regular instruction in learning to sing songs only in usual modes and nontonal songs perform nontonal songs better than children who receive regular instruction in learning to sing nontonal songs and songs in usual modes in addition to songs in unusual modes?

METHODS, PROCEDURES, AND DESIGN OF THE STUDY

Subjects

Eight hundred fifty-nine children enrolled in the Iowa City Community School District in 1971 initially participated in the study. These children constituted thirty-eight separate classes.

Teaching Procedure

In addition to the instruction in music as outlined in the Iowa City Community School District's *Music Curriculum Guide*, all subjects received special music instruction, relevant to this investigation, for three twenty-minute periods each week from February 1971 to June 1972. Tonal and rhythm activities were stressed equally. Overall, children participated in tonal and rhythmic activities designed generally to develop aural perception and kinesthetic reactions. Every music class was taught by elementary music specialists.

Experimental Groups

Each of the thirty-eight classes was randomly designated to serve in one of six experimental groups. As indicated in Table 1:

Table 1

Types of Tonal Instruction Offered
To Each of Six Experimental Groups

\	\	Experimental Groups	\	\	\
I	II	III	IV	V	VI
\	\	Types of Instruction Offered	\	\	\
major	major	major	major	major	major
minor	minor	minor	minor	minor	minor
	Dorian	Dorian	Lydian	Dorian	nontonal
	Phrygian	Phrygian	Mixolydian	Phrygian	
		Lydian		Lydian	
		Mixolydian		Mixolydian	
				nontonal	

1. Children in Experimental Group I received regular instruction in learning to sing songs in usual modes (major and minor).
2. Children in Experimental Group II received regular instruction in learning to sing songs in usual modes (major and minor) and minor related unusual modes (Dorian and Phrygian).
3. Children in Experimental Group III received regular instruction in learning to sing songs in usual modes (major and minor) and major related unusual modes (Lydian and Mixolydian).

4. Children in Experimental Group IV received regular instruction in learning to sing songs in all usual modes (major and minor) and unusual modes (Dorian, Phrygian, Lydian, and Mixolydian).
5. Children in Experimental Group V received regular instruction in learning to sing songs in all usual modes (major and minor) and unusual modes (Dorian, Phrygian, Lydian, and Mixolydian) in addition to nontonal songs.
6. Children in Experimental Group VI received regular instruction in learning to sing songs in usual modes (major and minor) and nontonal songs.

So that children in Experimental Groups II, III, IV, V, and VI could learn to perform songs in usual modes and/or nontonal songs, they spent a reduced amount of time on songs in usual modes compared to the time spent by children in Experimental Group I. Analogously, the children in Experimental Groups IV and V studied songs in all unusual modes and/or nontonal songs at the expense of time spent on songs in usual and unusual modes and/or nontonal songs.

Achievement Criteria

Each of the seven songs[15] adapted by the writer to serve as criterion performance measures was eight measures in length. When necessary, each song was rewritten in triple meter to minimize the effect different meters might have on the tonal performance measures. The seven songs comprised a similar range and tessitura and each was adapted to include the following tonal patterns: (1) upward and downward leaps, (2) repeated notes, and (3) upward and downward steps. With the exception of the nontonal song, each song was in one of the following modes: major, minor, Dorian, Phrygian, Lydian, and Mixolydian, as indicated in Table 2.

Procedures for Teaching Criterion Songs

After one and one-half years of instruction, the children were taught each criterion song on five successive days. Five minutes of each regularly scheduled twenty-minute music period were allotted to teach the song. The children in each experimental group were taught one criterion song in each mode in which they received regular instruction. For example, children in Experimental Group I were taught one criterion song in the major mode and one in the minor mode, while children in Experimental Group II were taught one criterion song in each of the following modes: major, minor, Dorian, and Phrygian. In order to allow one music period for tape recording individual performance, the teaching and tape recording of each of the seven criterion songs required two weeks, the equivalent of six music periods.

Table 2

Title and Mode of Songs
Used as Achievement Criteria

SONG	MODE	SONG TITLE
	Usual	
1	major	My Fiddle
2	minor	Hoppy, the Kangaroo
	Unusual Minor Related	
3	Dorian	Baby Alligator
4	Phrygian	Robot
	Unusual Major Related	
5	Lydian	Jingle Sticks
6	Mixolydian	The Gas Station
7	Nontonal	The Delivery Boy

The following methods of rote instruction were used by the music specialists to teach the criteria songs to the children. First, children only listened to the song. They then echoed each phrase of the song immediately after it was sung by the teacher. Finally, children sang the complete song after the teacher established the tempo, meter, tonality (when appropriate), and beginning pitch. Children learned to sing characteristic tonal patterns[16] which were extracted from the song. As children were learning the song, they were given an opportunity to perform the song individually and in small groups.

Tape Recording of Achievement Criteria

First, the songs were performed by the children in each group as a whole. Then the music teacher identified each child by an arbitrary number and established the correct tempo, meter, tonality (when appropriate), and beginning pitch of the song before each individual's performance was tape recorded.

Evaluation of Achievement Criteria

Evaluation of children's tape recorded performances of each criterion song was made by two elementary music specialists through the use of a seven-point rating scale, as described in Table 3. The evaluation materials given to each judge included the songs in notational form, a rating scale, a description of the musical task to be evaluated, the numerical identification of the children whose performances were on each tape, and the digital counter reference numbers for the location of each individual's performance on each tape.

Table 3

Rating Scale Used for the Evaluation
Of Children's Tape Recorded Performances*

SCALE	TONAL ACHIEVEMENT
1	Over-all poor tonal performance
2	No, or very poor, sense of tonality, but sense of direction
3	Poor sense of tonality, general sense of direction
4	Fair (moderately good) sense of tonality, good sense of direction
5	Good sense of tonality, very good sense of direction
6	Very good sense of tonality, very good sense of direction
7	Excellent tonal performance

*This rating scale was used for evaluating children's performances of all criterion songs including criterion Song 7, which was nontonal. A child's sense of "tonality" when performing the nontonal song was imputed according to his subjective feeling of a tonic as opposed to his objective determination of a tonic when performing all other criterion songs. For a more detailed explanation of this concept, see: Edwin Gordon, *The Psychology of Music Teaching* (Englewood Cliffs, N.J.: Prentice-Hall, 1971), p. 91.

Each judge independently recorded his evaluations of the children's performances of the criterion songs on separate rating sheets for each song. Through this procedure neither judge was influenced by his own ratings of a child's previous performances (which were in random order on the various tapes) nor by the ratings of the other judge.

The composite of the two judges' ratings was used to derive an over-all rating for each child's performance of each individual song. Thus, it was possible for a child to earn a minimum of two points or a maximum of fourteen points for each criterion song performed.

Statistical Design and Analysis

The individual group and the composite reliabilities of the two judges' ratings (interjudge reliability) were estimated for the children's performances of each criterion song. Also, the means and standard deviations of the individual judges' ratings were determined for each of the seven criterion songs.

To evaluate the comparative achievement of the children in the different experimental groups, a simple randomized design[17] was employed. Analysis of variance techniques were used to investigate the significance of the mean differences among the experimental groups for each of the seven criterion measures at the 5 per cent level of confidence. There were six experimental groups (see Table 1), and seven criterion measures (see Table 2) used in the study. The design was completed seven times, once for each of the seven criterion measures. However, not all six experimental groups were involved in each of the seven analyses. For example, as indicated in Table 4, the analysis of the nontonal criterion measure included only Experimental Groups V and VI, while the analysis of the criterion measure for the Dorian mode included Experimental Groups II, IV, and V.

PRESENTATION AND INTERPRETATION OF THE DATA

Two hundred seventy-one children of the eight hundred fifty-nine who initially participated in the study moved from the Iowa City Community School District or moved to a school in which the children had been previously assigned to a different experimental group. Therefore, data on five hundred eighty-eight children were available for analysis at the completion of the study.

Table 4

Experimental Groups Used in the Analysis
Of Each of the Seven Criterion Measures

CRITERION MEASURE		EXPERIMENTAL GROUPS					
Song	Mode						
1	major	I	II	III	IV	V	VI
2	minor	I	II	III	IV	V	VI
3	Dorian	–	II	–	IV	V	–
4	Phrygian	–	II	–	IV	V	–
5	Lydian	–	–	III	IV	V	–
6	Mixolydian	–	–	III	IV	V	–
7	nontonal	–	–	–	–	V	VI

Reliability of the Judges' Ratings

Table 5 contains the estimated reliability for the ratings on each song within each group and for the composite rating of each song. (The composite rating is average rating of the two judges for a recorded performance.) The lowest reliability coefficient is .91 and the highest .98. This indicates that the judges were very consistent in their evaluations. In comparing the composite reliabilities, it can be seen that the judges were in the highest agreement for Songs 6, 7, and 4, and were in least agreement for Songs 5, 3, 1, and 2. That the judges agreed so well can be attributed to the fact that both have taught in the same school system for four years and they had also served as an evaluation team on a previous study.

Analysis of Achievement Criteria

Song 1 — Major Mode

Performance score means and standard deviations for Song 1 in the major mode are presented in Table 6.

Table 5

Reliability of the Judges' Ratings of
Children's Tape Recorded Performances
Of the Seven Criterion Songs

Experimental Groups	CRITERION SONGS						
	1	2	3	4	5	6	7
I	.95	.93					
II	.95	.96	.96	.97			
III	.94	.95			.97	.97	
IV	.94	.91	.95	.95	.93	.96	
V	.96	.91	.95	.96	.97	.98	.96
VI	.95	.95					.97
Composite	.95	.94	.95	.96	.95	.97	.96

It can be seen in Table 6 that children who received regular instruction in learning to sing songs in major related unusual modes in addition to songs in usual modes (Experimental Group III) had the highest observed mean. Conversely, the children who received regular instruction in learning to sing songs only in usual modes and nontonal songs (Experimental Group VI) had the lowest observed mean. It would seem that when as much as one-third of instructional time is devoted to learning to sing nontonal songs (Experimental Group VI) as opposed to one-seventh of instructional time as experienced by

[85]

Table 6

Performance Score Means and Standard Deviations
For Criterion Song 1 in the Major Mode

EXPERIMENTAL GROUPS

I			II			III			IV			V			VI			Total		
M	SD	N	M	SD	N	M	SD	N	M	SD	N	M	SD	N	M	SD	N	M	SD	N
8.42	3.17	65	7.84	3.60	105	8.67	3.09	99	8.27	3.16	108	8.25	3.29	105	7.36	3.32	106	8.11	3.31	588

Summary Table

Source	df	ms	F-ratio
Groups	5	21.81	2.00*
Within	582	10.90	
Total	587		

*Not significant at the five per cent level. F_{05} (5,582) > 2.21

children in Experimental Group V, more generous exposure to nontonal music may hinder children's ability to perform songs in the major mode. However, because the main effect in the statistical analysis was not significant for this criterion, as indicated in Table 6, the foregoing interpretation cannot be objectified.

Considering the power (the large number of children participating in the study) and the precision (the high interjudge reliabilities) inherent in the analysis to discover a significant difference if in fact one did exist, it can be assumed that children who receive regular instruction in learning to sing songs only in usual modes do not perform songs in the major mode better than children who receive regular instruction in learning to sing songs in unusual modes and/or nontonal songs in addition to songs in the usual modes. Conversely, neither do the data indicate that regular instruction in learning to sing songs in unusual modes and/or nontonal songs in addition to songs in usual modes hinder children's ability to perform songs in the major mode.

Song 2 — Minor Mode

The performance score means for the criterion song in the minor mode presented in Table 7 indicate that performance of the minor mode song was affected by the six variations in instructional time devoted to learning to sing songs in usual and unusual modes and/or nontonal songs. Highest average performance scores were recorded by the children in Experimental Group I who received regular instruction in learning to sing songs only in usual modes. The children who received regular instruction in learning to sing songs in usual modes and nontonal songs (Experimental Group VI) had the lowest observed mean. Because the main effect in the statistical analysis was significant for this criterion, Winer's adaptation (for groups of unequal numbers) of Tukey's method for testing the significance of simple effects was utilized.[18] The results of this analysis are presented in Table 8. A significant difference was found between the mean scores of the children who received regular instruction in learning to sing songs only in usual modes (Experimental Group I) and the children who received regular instruction in learning to sing songs in usual modes and nontonal songs (Experimental Group VI). Also, a significant difference was discovered between the mean scores of children who received regular instruction in learning to sing songs in major related unusual modes in addition to songs in usual modes (Experimental Group III) and the children in Experimental Group VI. These data indirectly substantiate the observed effect reported for criterion song one. That is, when one-third of instructional time is devoted to learning to sing nontonal songs as opposed to one-seventh of instructional time, additional exposure to nontonal music may hinder children's ability to perform songs in usual modes.

Table 7

Performance Score Means and Standard Deviations
For Criterion Song 2 in the Minor Mode

EXPERIMENTAL GROUPS

I			II			III			IV			V			VI			Total		
M	SD	N	M	SD	N	M	SD	N	M	SD	N	M	SD	N	M	SD	N	M	SD	N
9.15	2.71	65	8.50	2.92	105	8.95	2.63	99	8.21	2.41	108	8.30	2.84	105	7.76	3.22	106	8.43	2.84	588

Summary Table

Source	df	ms	F-ratio
Groups	5	23.07	2.90*
Within	582	7.96	
Total	587		

*Significant at the five per cent level. F_{05} (5, 582) > 2.21

Table 8

Significance Tests of the Mean Differences Among the Six
Treatment Groups for Song 2 in the Minor Mode

Experimental Groups		VI	IV	V	II	III	I
	Means	7.76	8.21	8.30	8.50	8.95	9.15
VI	7.76	–	0.45	0.54	0.74	1.19*	1.39*
IV	8.21		–	0.09	0.29	0.74	0.94
V	8.30			–	0.20	0.65	0.85
II	8.50				–	0.45	0.65
III	8.95					–	0.20
I	9.15						–

*Significant at q_{95} (94) > 1.18

Song 3 — Dorian Mode

The analysis of the means presented in Table 9 reveals no significant differences. It may be noted, however, from the observed means that children who received regular instruction in learning to sing songs in all usual and unusual modes (Experimental Group IV) performed the criterion song in the Dorian mode best. The children who received regular instruction in learning to sing nontonal songs in addition to songs in all usual and unusual modes (Experimental Group V) had the lowest observed mean.

Table 9

Performance Score Means and Standard Deviations
For Criterion Song 3 in the Dorian Mode

EXPERIMENTAL GROUPS

II			IV			V			Total		
M	SD	N	M	SD	N	M	SD	N	M	SD	N
8.96	3.23	105	9.33	2.90	108	8.66	3.06	105	8.99	3.08	318

Summary Table

Source	df	ms	F-ratio
Groups	2	12.22	1.29*
Within	315	9.48	
Total	317		

*Not significant at the five per cent level. F_{05} (2,315) > 3.03

Song 4 — Phrygian Mode

The data presented in Table 10 for Song 4 in the Phrygian mode indicate that children who received regular instruction in learning to sing songs in minor related unusual modes in addition to songs in usual modes (Experimental Group II) had the highest observed mean. As was found for the criterion song in the Dorian mode, the children who received regular instruction in learning to sing songs in all usual and unusual modes as well as nontonal songs (Experimental Group V) had the lowest observed mean. The consistency of the lowest mean to be associated with Experimental Group V tends to suggest that exposure to nontonal music may inhibit children's ability to perform songs in a usual mode or a minor related unusual mode. However, as indicated in the analysis of variance summary presented in Table 10, the differences among the mean scores were not significant for this criterion.

Song 5 — Lydian Mode

Performance score means for criterion Song 5 in the Lydian mode are presented in Table 11.

The data favored children who received regular instruction in learning to sing songs in usual modes and major related unusual modes (Experimental Group III). The lowest mean was for the children who received regular instruction in learning to sing songs in all usual and unusual modes as well as nontonal songs (Experimental Group V). Similar to the results for previous criteria, the fact that the lowest mean score is again associated with Experimental Group V tends to suggest that exposure to nontonal music may adversely affect children's ability to perform songs in the Lydian mode. However, these interpretations must be viewed as very tenuous because the main effect in the statistical analysis was not significant.

Table 10

Performance Score Means and Standard Deviations
For Criterion Song 4 in the Phrygian Mode

EXPERIMENTAL GROUPS

II			IV			V			Total		
M	SD	N	M	SD	N	M	SD	N	M	SD	N
8.15	3.67	105	7.49	2.85	108	7.25	3.29	105	7.63	3.31	318

Summary Table

Source	df	ms	F-ratio
Groups	2	23.05	2.12*
Within	315	10.88	
Total	317		

*Not significant at the five per cent level. F_{05} (2,315) > 3.03

Table 11

Performance Score Means and Standard Deviations
For Criterion Song 5 in the Lydian Mode

EXPERIMENTAL GROUPS

III			IV			V			Total		
M	SD	N	M	SD	N	M	SD	N	M	SD	N
8.48	2.76	99	8.31	2.98	108	7.95	3.19	105	8.25	3.00	312

Summary Table

Source	df	ms	F-ratio
Groups	2	7.61	0.84*
Within	309	9.01	
Total	311		

*Not significant at the five per cent level. F_{05} (2,309) > 3.03

Song 6 — Mixolydian Mode

An examination of the observed performance score means presented in Table 12 suggest that children who received regular instruction in learning to sing songs in all usual and unusual modes (Experimental Group IV) performed the Mixolydian criterion song better than children who received instruction in all usual and unusual modes as well as nontonal songs (Experimental Group V).

Contrary to the observed results for previous analyses, Experimental Group V did not have the lowest observed mean in this analysis. The lowest observed mean was for the children who received instruction in usual modes and major related unusual modes (Experimental Group III). These observed effects might suggest that limited exposure to nontonal music is not detrimental to learning to sing songs in the Mixolydian mode. However, the main effect in the statistical analysis was not significant for this criterion.

Table 12

Peformance Score Means and Standard Deviations
for Criterion Song 6 in the Mixolydian Mode

EXPERIMENTAL GROUPS

III			IV			V			Total		
M	SD	N	M	SD	N	M	SD	N	M	SD	N
8.75	3.09	99	9.23	3.04	108	8.85	3.67	39	8.98	3.18	246

Summary Table

Source	df	ms	F-ratio
Groups	2	6.43	0.63*
Within	243	10.15	
Total	245		

*Not significant at the five per cent level. F_{05} (2,243) > 3.04

Song 7 — Nontonal

Performance score means and standard deviations for Song 7, which was nontonal, are presented in Table 13.

It may be noted that the children who received regular instruction in learning to sing songs in all usual and unusual modes as well as nontonal songs (Experimental Group V) had the highest observed mean. The lowest observed mean was for the children who received regular instruction in learning to sing songs only in usual modes and nontonal songs (Experimental Group VI). It is interesting to note that difference between the observed means, although negligible, for these two experimental groups tends to suggest that excessive exposure to nontonal music may hinder children's ability to perform nontonal songs. However, the main effect for this analysis was not significant.

Table 13

Performance Score Means and Standard Deviations
for Criterion Song 7 — Nontonal

EXPERIMENTAL GROUPS

V			VI			Total		
M	SD	N	M	SD	N	M	SD	N
7.55	3.41	105	7.47	3.43	106	7.51	3.42	211

Summary Table

Source	df	ms	F-ratio
Groups	1	0.34	0.03*
Within	209	11.81	
Total	210		

*Not significant at the five per cent level. F_{05} (1,209) > 3.89

Conclusions of the Study

On the basis of the results of this study, it may be concluded that young children are generally able to profit from instruction which includes the singing of songs in the Dorian, Phrygian, Lydian, and Mixolydian modes in addition to songs which are in the major and minor modes. Also, although further research is needed for substantiation, it may be tentatively concluded that excessive exposure to nontonal music (as much as one-third of instructional time) may inhibit children's ability to sing nontonal songs. However, limited exposure (as little as one-seventh of instructional time) to nontonal music might aid children in learning to sing nontonal songs.

APPENDIX

SONGS USED FOR EVALUATION

Song 1 — Major Mode

My Fiddle

American Book Company
Kindergarten Book
Adapted by P. Miller

Song 2 — Minor Mode

Hoppy, the Kangaroo

American Book Company
Kindergarten Book
Adapted by P. Miller

Song 3 — Dorian Mode

Baby Alligator

American Book Company
Kindergarten Book
Adapted by P. Miller

Song 4 — Phrygian Mode

Robot

American Book Company
Kindergarten Book
Adapted by P. Miller

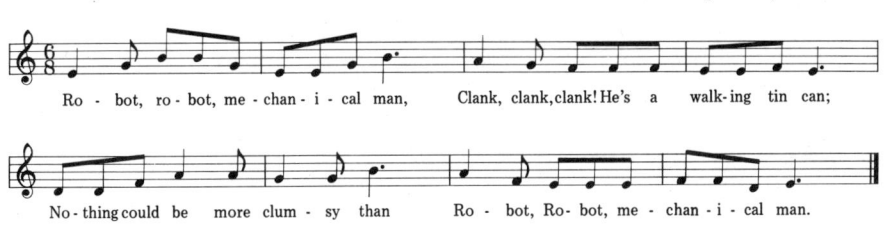

Song 5 — Lydian Mode

Jingle Sticks

American Book Company
Kindergarten Book
Adapted by P. Miller

Song 6 — Mixolydian

The Gas Station

American Book Company
First Grade Book
Adapted by P. Miller

Song 7 — Nontonal

The Delivery Boy

American Book Company
Kindergarten Book
Adapted by P. Miller

Knock, knock, knock,   Knock, knock, knock,   Who's knock-ing at the door?

Knock, knock, knock,   Knock, knock, knock, The boy from the gro-c'ry store.

Notes

Philip H. Miller is chairman of the Music Department, School District No. 102, LaGrange Park, Illinois.

1   Music Educators National Conference, *The Study of Music in the Elementary School: A Conceptual Approach* (Washington, D.C.: Music Educators National Conference, 1967), pp. 51–66.
2   Music written in the major or minor mode.
3   Music written in any of the following modes: Dorian, Phrygian, Lydian, or Mixolydian.
4   Music which suggests more than one pitch, or possibly no pitch at all, at a tonic.
5   Robert House, "Curriculum Construction in Music Education," *Basic Concepts in Music Education*, ed. Nelson B. Henry (Chicago: University of Chicago Press, 1958), p. 248.
6   Leonard B. Meyer, *Music, The Arts, and Ideas: Patterns and Predictions in Twentieth-Century Culture* (Chicago: University of Chicago Press, 1967), p. 274.
7   Meyer, p. 176.
8   John Pfeiffer, *The Human Brain* (New York: Pyramid Publications, 1962), pp. 42–43.
9   Meyer, p. 176.
10   Meyer, p. 175.
11   James L. Mursell, "Growth Processes in Music Education," *Basic Concepts in Music Education*, ed. Nelson B. Henry (Chicago: University of Chicago Press, 1958), p. 157.
12   Mursell, pp. 158–159.
13   Robert M. De Yarman, "An Experimental Analysis of the Development of Rhythmic and Tonal Capabilities of Kindergarten and First Grade Children," *Experimental Research in the Psychology of Music: 8*, Studies in the Psychology of Music, Vol. 8 (Iowa City: University of Iowa Press, 1972), pp. 1–44.
14   Iowa City Community School District, *Music Curriculum Guide* (Iowa City: Iowa City Community School District, 1971).
15   The seven songs may be found in notational form in the Appendix.
16   Characteristic tonal patterns consist of two or three notes that are functions of the mode of the song. For example, major and minor tonal patterns are primarily based on tonic, dominant, dominant seventh, and subdominant harmonic functions, while characteristic tonal patterns in unusual modes usually contain the note that makes it different from either the major or natural minor mode as the case may be. For example, Dorian tonal patterns would include a raised sixth, the note that differentiates this mode from the natural minor mode.
17   E. F. Lindquist, *Design and Analysis of Experiments in Psychology and Education* (Boston: Houghton Mifflin, 1953), pp. 47–101.
18   B. J. Winer, *Statistical Principles in Experimental Design* (New York: McGraw-Hill, 1962), pp. 77–85.

AN INVESTIGATION TO DETERMINE WHETHER LEARNING EFFECTS ACCRUE FROM IMMEDIATE SEQUENTIAL ADMINISTRATIONS OF THE SIX LEVELS OF THE *IOWA TESTS OF MUSIC LITERACY*

Thelma Volger

Introduction

Concern with objectivity in measurement of students' academic progress has been reflected in many disciplines in development of standardized tests of achievement. Beyond their obvious and important uses to objectively measure students' achievement and provide assurance of effective teaching, statistical features of standardized tests enable educators to utilize results to comparatively evaluate teaching methods, to determine sequential objectives, and even to examine processes of learning which are unique to a discipline. During the past decade, complaints against the discipline of music education have been related to a dearth of standardized tests of musical achievement.

This limitation, which contributes to the possibility of overlooking early development and continued encouragement of musically talented students, has been the expressed concern of prominent music educators. In recent publications, both Whybrew and Lehman refer to the need for standardized tests of musical achievement.[1,2] Whybrew suggests that this scarcity is probably due to the subjective nature of music curricula;[3] a subjective nature frequently expressed in nonquantifiable terms such as enjoyment or appreciation. According to Lehman, there has been a ". . . lack of consensus among music teachers as to what specific outcomes should be expected as a result of instruction in music. Concurrently, there has been a lack of agreement on what specific musical experiences and activities should constitute the curriculum, for one can scarcely know how to proceed if he has not identified his goal."[4] Gordon states that objective measures are required to effectively evaluate an individual student's growth in musical achievement in relation to his capacity for potential development, ". . . in order to enhance his strengths, while compensating for those areas in which he is deficient."[5] Meanwhile, over-all aspects of music education emphasize and culminate in performance groups for relatively small portions of student bodies. Problems attendant upon non-use of objective measures — selection of students, drop-out rates, and performance standards — are largely related to the ability to read musical notation. Evidence of creative use of musical notation is practically nonexistent.

The problem was succinctly stated in a report from a seminar held in 1963 at Yale University on the topic, "Music in Our Schools, A Search for Improvement."[6] A specific complaint against music education might be construed to represent the goal which members of the seminar, professional musicians, music educators, and guests from other disciplines envisioned for music education:

> Even in students who are potentially gifted and intellectually capable, creativity and agility of musical thought and judgment are left almost entirely undeveloped, while fingers and lips are drilled to a considerable speed and accuracy. [And] . . . feverish and massive activity . . . somehow does not produce that essential attribute of the musician and perceptive listener — the capacity to hear internally a musical line.[7]

The consensus that a model curriculum should be developed for music education was tempered by the statement that this curriculum would depend for its success upon careful evaluative techniques.

> The first phase of this evaluation will depend upon devising tests, both achievement and predictive, a difficult task in an area where tests have been a stumbling block because of the non-verbal nature of the subject.[8]

Undoubtedly, the "non-verbal nature" of music has exacerbated the problem of test development in music education, preventing establishment of clearly identified objectives upon which members of the profession might have a basis for concurrence.[9] That is, identification, such as Bruner advocates, of "underlying structure" has been deterred in the discipline of music education largely because verbal terminology in common use has been insufficient to identify and communicate such structural objectives.[10] In specific reference to insufficiency of verbal terminology for study of rhythm, Cooper and Meyer state: "The development of a fruitful approach to the study of rhythm has been hampered by failure to distinguish clearly among the serveral aspects of temporal organization itself. The resulting confusion has created a correlative ambiguity of terminology."[11]

The expression "non-verbal nature" acknowledges a parallelism between the disciplines of "language arts" and music. In *The Psychology of Music Teaching*, Gordon draws such a parallel, intuitively identifying musical patterns as basic units of perception in music — "words" in the language of music. He elaborates on the development of a "vocabulary" of patterns[12] analogous to development of language, suggesting separate attention to tone patterns and rhythm patterns. Frequently, terms related to perceptual organization or to categories of patterns are supplied by the author. Based on his "vocabulary" of tone patterns and rhythm patterns, Gordon has developed a battery of objective measures of musical achievement, simple to complex in difficulty.

Recently published by The University of Iowa, the *Iowa Tests of Music Literacy*,[13] (*ITML*),[14] comprise six Levels designed to measure sequential development of *Tonal Concepts* and *Rhythmic Concepts* "that form a foundation for music literacy."[15] In their original form of *ITML* Levels had been devised as longitudinal validity criteria for the test author's first publication, the *Musical Aptitude Profile*,[16] (*MAP*).[17] In *MAP*, Gordon established three objectively measurable dimensions of musical aptitude: *Tonal Imagery*; *Rhythm Imagery*; and *Musical Sensitivity*. *ITML* measures of musical achievement correspond to the two dimensions of musical aptitude visually symbolized in musical notation, tone and rhythm. Objectives designated in separate divisions of *ITML* Levels are embodied within the tone patterns or rhythm patterns of which test items are comprised. Implicit in the sequential Levels of *ITML* is the outline of a curriculum for music education. In the words of the test author, ". . . the structure of a comprehensive test could serve as a curricular guide before the battery is used for evaluative purposes."[18]

All Levels of *ITML* are designed with identical subtests corresponding to three stages of the learning process. The author states specifically:

> Fundamental musical achievement comprises tonal and rhythmic aural perception (the ability to distinguish mode and meter when listening to music) and tonal and rhythmic literacy (the ability to musically hear and feel what one reads and writes in notational form).[19]

Subtests titled *Aural Perception, Reading Recognition,* and *Notational Understanding,* are abbreviated: T_1, T_2, and T_3; and R_1, R_2, and R_3. In each division the first subtest is a measure of ability to discriminate between two options of mode or meter.[20] The second and third subtests are measures of literacy skills; *Reading Recognition* requires visual identification of tonal or rhythmic symbols; *Notational Understanding* also requires written use of tonal or rhythmic notation. The same tone patterns or rhythm patterns are utilized in items for the first two subtests of a division at each Level; patterns are identified aurally in T_1 or R_1 and visually in T_2 or R_2. In deference to more exacting requirements of the third subtest, items for T_3 or R_3 are comprised either of less complex patterns or less advanced literacy skills than are demanded for subtests T_2 and R_2.

Regarding use of the battery, the author states:

> The value of a test is determined by the extent to which its use improves and develops individual talent. To these ends the *Iowa Tests of Music Literacy* may be used for the following four specific purposes:

(1) to diagnose a student's individual strengths and weaknesses in six different dimensions of tonal and rhythmic aural perception and music literacy achievement.
(2) to compare a student's tonal and rhythmic aural perception and music literacy achievement to his musical potential, as measured by the *Musical Aptitude Profile*.
(3) to evaluate the extent of a student's continuous development from simple to complex tonal and rhythmic aural perception and music literacy achievement.
(4) to determine a student's relative standing among other students in tonal and rhythmic aural perception and music literacy achievement.[21]

Musical objectives identified in the six Levels of *ITML* as embodied within test items are presented in Figures 1 and 2.

The test author's explanations of terms to categorize mode and meter used in the *Iowa Tests of Music Literacy*, and found in Figures 1 and 2, quoted from *The Psychology of Music Teaching*, are included immediately following Figures 1 and 2.

Figure 1 — Tonal Concepts

A. *Aural Perception*, T_1

Sequential Organization of Tonal Patterns in
The Subtests of *Aural Perception*, $\dot{T}_1$, in the
Six Levels of *ITML*

Level	Response Options (also "In-Doubt")		Pattern Difficulty
1	Major — Minor	Basic — Basic	Unison
2	Major — Minor	Complex — Complex	Unison
3	Usual — Unusual	Complex — Basic	Unison
4	Usual — Unusual	Complex — Basic	Unison

[101]

	Major	Complex	Two-Voice
5	—	—	Counterpoint
	Minor	Complex	or Dyads
	Major	Complex	Harmony:
6	—	—	Chordal
	Minor	Complex	Accompaniment

The terms "basic" and "complex" were adopted for this study because basic implies the fundamental organization of patterns in relation to a classification or category of tonality. The term complex implies the complex nature of some of the patterns as they are organized in the Levels of *ITML*. See Gordon, *The Psychology of Music Teaching*, p. 97.

B. Definition of Terms

Definition of Terms for Tonal Concepts as
They Are Applied to the Tonal Patterns
Used in the Sequential Levels of *ITML*

Basic Major: Tonal patterns comprised of tones which are primarily related to tonic, dominant, dominant-seventh or sub-dominant functions, with passing tones, and which begin or end on "do."

Basic Minor: Same as above, derived from harmonic minor, and which begin or end on "la."

Complex Major or Minor: Addition to above of tones from the appropriate mediant or submediant functions, also key-related intervals, as in temporary modulations.

Usual: Tonal patterns which are in the familiar tonalities of major or minor modes.

Unusual: In Level 3, the term is applied to tonal patterns in less familiar modes. (Used as a response option in subtest T_1.)

Basic Modal: Tonal patterns comprised of tones which are functions of dorian, phrygian, lydian, and mixolydian modes. Modal patterns include the characteristic tones (dorian — raised 6th; phrygian — lowered 2nd; lydian — raised 4th; mixolydian — lowered 7th) and end on their respective resting tones.

Unusual: In Level 4, the term is applied to tonal patterns without an objective resting tone. (Used as a response option in subtest T_1.)

Basic Unusual: Tonal patterns comprised of tones which are chromatic embellishments outside of familiar or modal tonalities.

Complex Unusual: Tonal patterns which are comprised of extensive use of chromatic embellishments and intervals outside of tonal functions, thus changing objective relationships to tonality and giving rise to nontonal patterns.

C. Reading Recognition, T_2

Sequential Organization of Literacy Skills in
The Subtests of *Reading Recognition*, T_2, in the
Six Levels of *ITML*

Level	Tonality	Clef	Key Signature	Accidentals
1	Major — Minor	𝄞	C major — A minor	Sharp
2	Major — Minor	𝄞	C major — A minor	Sharp Flat
3	Usual — Modal	𝄞	C, G, D, A, F, B♭, E♭	Sharp Flat Natural
4	Usual — Nontonal	𝄞 𝄢	C, G, D, A, F, B♭ E♭	Sharp, Flat Natural Double Sharp Double Flat
5	Major — Minor	𝄞 𝄢	C, G, D, A, F, B♭ E♭	Sharp Flat Natural
6	Major — Minor	𝄞	C, G_7, F Chords a, E_7, d	Sharp Flat

The tonal patterns heard in subtest T_1 are transferred to visual symbols in subtest T_2. The student is asked only to recognize whether the tonal notation that he sees represents what he hears (Yes) or is different (No). The "In-Doubt" response option is also offered. Test items may differ in direction or in size of interval.

D. *Notational Understanding*, T_3

Sequential Organization of Literacy Skills in
The Subtests of *Notational Understanding*, T_3, in the
Six Levels of *ITML*

Level	Tonality	Clef	Key Signature	Accidentals
1	Major — Minor	𝄞	C major — A minor	Sharp
2	Major — Minor	𝄞	C major — A minor	Sharp Flat
3	Usual — Modal	𝄞	F, E, A, C Usual Modal	Sharp Flat Natural
4	Usual — Nontonal	𝄢	G, B♭, A, D, C Usual Nontonal	Sharp Flat Natural
5	Nontonal	𝄞	F♯ B♭	Sharp, Flat Natural Double Sharp
6	Usual — Nontonal	𝄞	C major A minor Nontonal	Sharp Flat Natural

In subtest T_3, the student both recognizes and uses tonal notation, completing a tonal pattern by choosing from two options on the answer sheet for each tone missing from the pattern he hears. Either the tonal concepts or the visual skills required are less complex in T_3 than those in T_2.

Figure 2 — Rhythmic Concepts

A. *Aural Perception*, R_1

Sequential Organization of Rhythm Patterns in
The Subtests of *Aural Perception*, R_1, in the
Six Levels of *ITML*

Level	Response Options (also "In-Doubt")	Pattern Difficulty
1	Duple	Basic
	—	—
	Triple	Basic
2	Duple	Complex
	—	—
	Triple	Complex
3	Usual	Complex
	—	—
	Mixed	Basic
4	Usual	Complex
	—	—
	Unusual	Basic
5	Mixed	Basic
	—	—
	Unusual	Basic
6	Mixed	Complex
	—	—
	Unusual	Complex

The terms "basic" and "complex" are applied to the Rhythmic Concepts of this study in a manner similar to their use for Tonal Concepts. See footnote, Figure 1.

B. Definition of Terms

Definition of Terms as Applied to Rhythm
Patterns Used in the Sequential Levels of
The *Iowa Tests of Music Literacy*

Basic Duple or Triple Meter: Rhythm patterns comprised of tempo beats, meter beats, fractionated and elongated meter beats, and their equivalent rests, also upbeats, dotted notes, and syncopations within the measure. Written with the meter signatures $^2_4$ or $^6_8$ to provide eighth note meter beats beamed in two's or three's.

Complex Duple Meter or Triple Meter: The addition to the above of elongated tempo beats and rests, a further subdivision of meter beats, the double dot, upbeats on a tempo beat, and ties — both within the measure and across bar lines. Also, meter signatures in which the quarter note represents the meter beat.

Basic Mixed Meter: Triplets or duplets, which are comprised only of meter beats, interpolated within duple meter or triple meter, respectively.

Complex Mixed Meter: Rhythm patterns comprised of dotted notes, rests, fractionations, elongations or syncopations within triplets or duplets.

Usual Meter: Meter perceived over regularly recurring tempo beats which are consistent in time, as with duple, triple, and mixed meter.

Unusual Meter: Meter characterized by the perception of temporally inconsistent or irregularly organized tempo beats, dependent upon the arbitrary grouping of meter beats.

Basic Unusual Meter: Groupings of meter beats in two's, three's, or single meter beats. Written with eighth notes, beamed in obvious groupings.

Complex Unusual Meter: Rhythm patterns of unusual meter beat groupings including dots, rests, fractionations, elongations, and syncopations or ties.

C. Reading Recognition, R_2

Sequential Organization of Literacy Skills in
The *Reading Recognition* Subtests, R_2, *ITML*

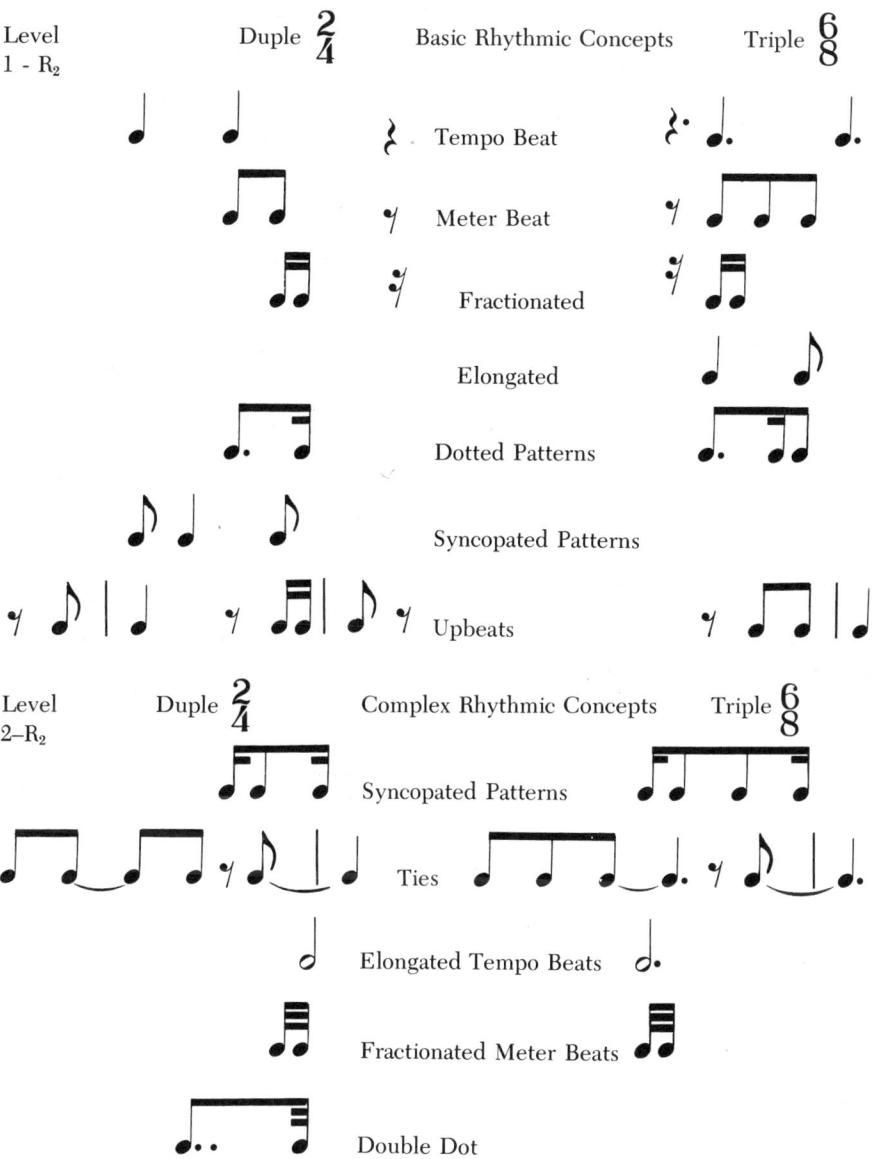

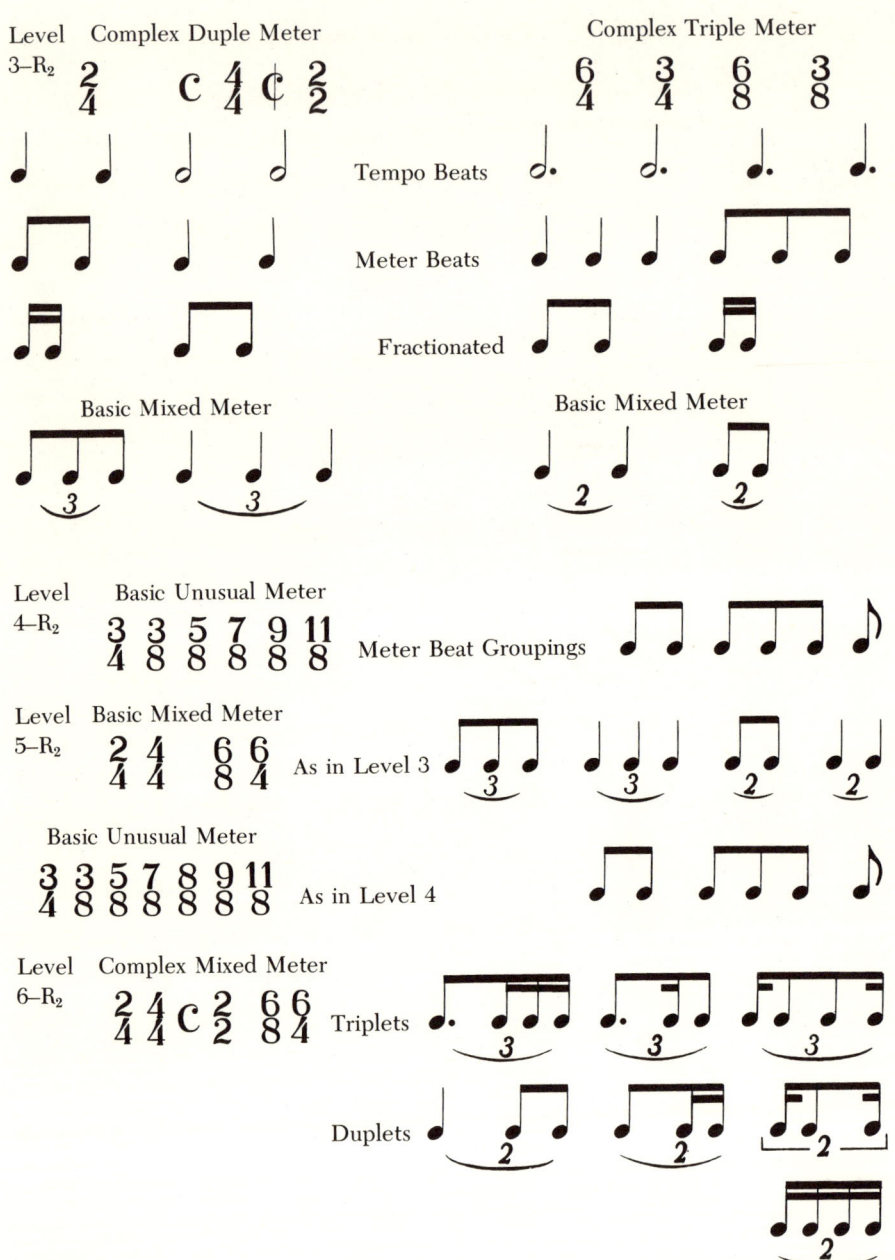

Complex Unusual Meter

3/4 3/8 5/8 7/8 9/8 11/8 Elongated Meter Beats

Ties

Dots

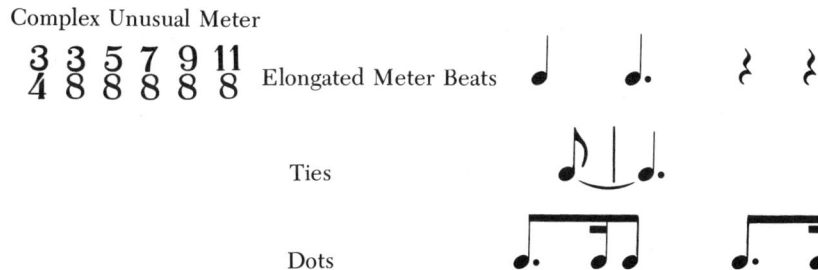

D. *Notational Understanding*, R_3

Sequential Organization of Literacy Skills in
The *Notational Understanding* Subtests, R_3, *ITML*

Level 1–R_3 | Duple 2/4 | Basic Rhythmic Concepts | Triple 6/8

 Tempo Beat

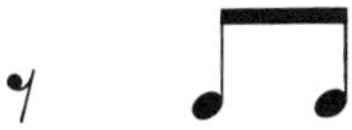

 Meter Beat

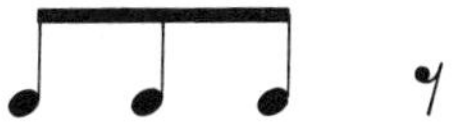

Elongated

Level 2–R_3 | Duple 2/4 | Complex Rhythmic Concepts | Triple 6/8

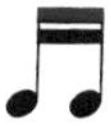

 Fractionated Meter Beat

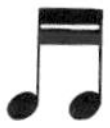

 Dotted Meter Beat

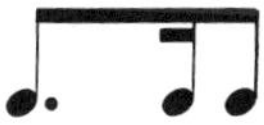

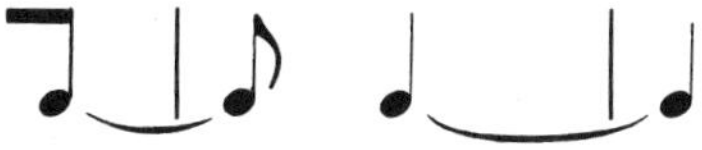

 Tie

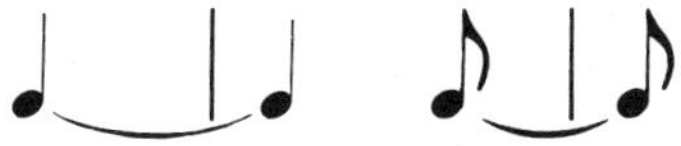

Level 3–R_3 | Duple 2/4 | Basic Mixed Meter | Triple 6/8

Triplet/Duplet

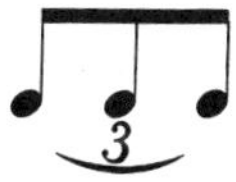

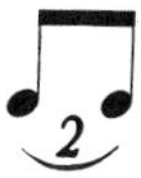

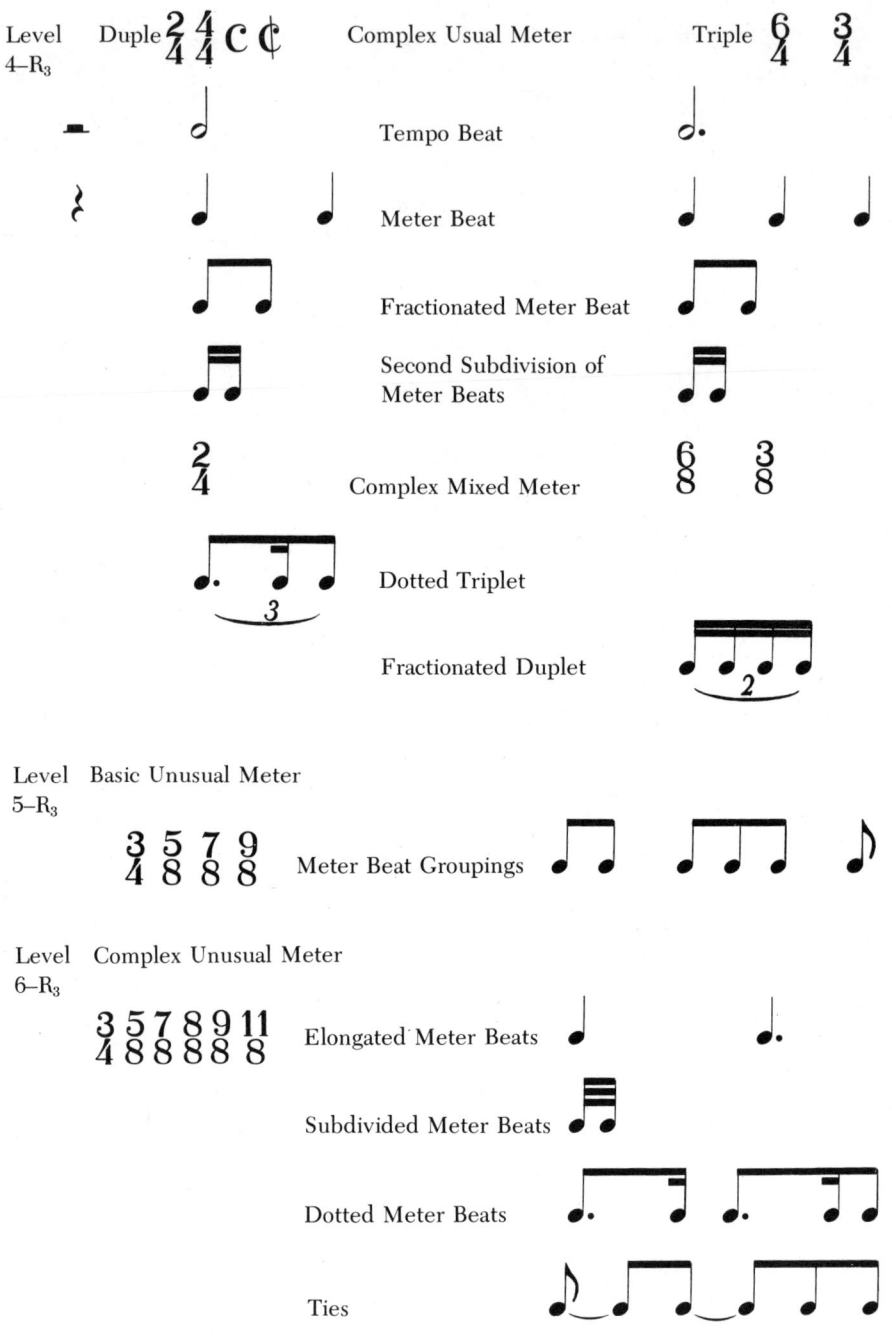

Explanation of Terms in Figures 1 and 2
(Used in the *Iowa Tests of Music Literacy**)

Tonal Concepts

Tonality — "A sense of tonality is established when tonal relationships suggest one tone (which may not even be comprised in the pattern) as being most restful; and from that objective resting tone, it can be established whether the music is major or minor, or in less familiar modal tonality." (P. 91.) "The terms 'major' and 'minor', like those of 'modal' and 'unusual', are referred to as types of tonality."

Tonal Pattern — "The ability to aurally perceive tonal patterns through musical imagery constitutes tonal reading readiness. Moreover, to be able to hear tonal relationships within and between patterns of tones represents evidence of one's ability to conceptualize musical sound, which is basic to musical enjoyment and understanding." (P. 91.)

Key — "The letter name of the resting note of a mode, determined by the key signature." (P. 97.)

Usual — "Although major and minor correspond to the Ionian and Aeolian modes, respectively, from practical usage, they are referred to as usual modes." (P. 97.)

Unusual — "Dorian, Phrygian, Lydian, Mixolydian, and Locrian, because of their less frequent use, are referred to as unusual modes." (P. 97.)

Unusual Tonality — "Patterns in unusual tonality bear no functional relationship to any mode and as a result, the 'tonality' which they suggest is not objective, but rather, a matter of subjective opinion. Therefore, they are termed nontonal." (P. 97.)

*All quotes are from the book, *The Psychology of Music Teaching*, except those few specifically indicated from the *Manual* of *ITML*.

Rhythmic Concepts

Meter — "Meter — in music, poetry, and speech — 'moves' in two's and three's." (P. 68.)

Tempo Beat — "Of the three basic elements of rhythm, tempo beats are fundamental because they provide the foundation upon which all other elements of rhythm are superimposed." "Rhythm is comprised of three basic elements. They are: (1) tempo beats, (2) meter beats, and (3) melodic rhythm. In music, these elements interact in a composite polyrhythmic manner and give rise to what is referred to as rhythm." (P. 68.)

Meter Beat — "Meter beats are of more importance to rhythm than tempo beats because when tempo beats are subjectively organized into pairs, meter is felt as a group of two beats (which gives rise to duple meter) or as a group of three beats (which gives rise to triple meter) within the duration of one each tempo beat."

Duple, Triple — "The terms 'duple' and 'triple', like those of 'mixed' and 'unusual', are referred to as types of meter. Patterns written in duple meter are those which generally have a 2 or 4 as the upper numeral of the meter signature. Patterns written in triple meter are those which generally have 3, 6, or 12 as the upper numeral of the meter signature." (P. 10.)

Rhythm Pattern — "Two or more notes or rests (in practical usage, up to six) which comprise a rhythm pattern in the mind of the listener, and which elicit musical meaning by the relationship among the three basic counterparts of rhythm." "Melodic rhythm patterns — which are superimposed on tempo beats $\frac{2}{4}$(♩ ♩) or $\frac{6}{8}$(♩. ♩.) and meter beats $\frac{2}{4}$(♫) or $\frac{6}{8}$(♫♫) and may be coincidental with or represent fractionations or elongations of tempo and meter beats — include at least two notes (or rests) and in practical usage, they comprise up to six notes (or rests)." (P. 67.)

Usual Meter — "Both duple and triple (meter) are considered usual meter." (P. 69.)

Mixed Meter — "Only duple and triple meter beats constitute basic mixed patterns. These patterns are used in conjunction with a contrasting duple or triple meter signature and they are notated as triplets or duplets $\frac{2}{4}$(♩♩♩), $\frac{6}{8}$ (♩.♩), respectively; this produces mixed meter." "Mixed meter patterns include triplets or duplets, but have numerals in the meter signature which designate duple or triple meter, respectively." (P. 10.)

Unusual Meter — "There are four types of basic unusual patterns:
  (1) those comprising just two tempo beats with meter beats grouped in two's and three's as in $\frac{5}{8}$ ♫ ♫♫
  (2) those comprising more than two tempo beats with meter beats grouped in two's and three's as in $\frac{11}{8}$ ♫♫ ♫ ♫♫ ♫♫
  (3) those comprising more than two tempo beats with some tempo beats void of meter as in $\frac{7}{8}$ ♪♫♫ ♫♪
  (4) those comprising three tempo beats with meter beats consistently grouped in either two's or three's as in $\frac{3}{4}$ ♫ ♫ ♫ and $\frac{9}{8}$ ♫♫ ♫♫ ♫♫

"Patterns written in unusual meter are generally those which have a 5, 7, 9, or 11 and sometimes a 3 as the upper numeral of the meter signature." (Gordon, *ITML Manual*, p. 10.)

Unusual Rhythm Patterns — "Unusual rhythm patterns differ from mixed rhythm patterns in two very important respects. First, in mixed meter (as in usual meter) tempo beats are consistent in time; — . . . conversely, in unusual meter, meter beats are not notated as duplets and triplets and therefore are consistent in time. Second, unusual patterns necessarily comprise a complete measure." (P. 71.)

Purpose and Problem of the Study

Whether it is feasible, even possible, to initiate new procedures and goals for upper-class students is a practical question with far-reaching consequences. The study reported in this article was initially undertaken as a practical consideration of questions which might arise in implementing the use of *ITML* for upper-class students not previously taught according to musical objectives delineated in the sequential content of the *ITML* battery. Of five validity-related studies completed since publication of *ITML*, those by Swindell, Mohatt, and Foss more specifically related to sequence of *ITML* Level objectives were antecedent to this study.[22-26] Directly concerned with test content, findings in three experimental studies, Dittemore, De Yarman, and Miller also bear on this study.[27,28,29]

Dittemore's investigation was similar to this study in that subjects were chosen to represent a well-structured program taught by music specialists, but who had not been formally trained to specific objectives measured. He investigated the receptiveness of students of varying musical aptitude at six grade levels, not including kindergarten, to twelve aspects of tonal and rhythmic concepts. In an attempt to suggest order and sequence for a music curriculum in relation to capability, selected concepts were presented through songs in successive weeks; four days of training and a final day of tape-recorded performance. His interesting rating scale on performance of songs was related to patterns. However, although he attempted to take into account the relative difficulty of patterns, there was no way to determine the interaction of elements other than the aspect being measured. That is, tonal concepts and rhythmic concepts were interacting in songs, rather than isolated for diagnostic purposes, as in subtests of *ITML*.

The De Yarman study dealt with students in kindergarten and first grade to whom he had given specific training over a school year in selected tonal and rhythmic concepts. De Yarman was concerned with the effect of beginning training, whether restriction to usual mode and meter might inhibit enlargement of categorical recognition so that early exposure to less familiar categories would be advantageous; or whether, through restriction for some period of time to usual mode and meter a frame of reference would be solidified so that comparison and contrast could be more secure. Also, the possibility of inherent difficulty among categories rather than unfamiliarity due to traditional teaching practices or cultural environment could appropriately be examined at such an early age. Investigation of tonal concepts was limited to tonal (major and harmonic minor) and nontonal. Rhythmic concepts included duple, triple, mixed and unusual meters. Evaluation of performance was based on songs adapted by De Yarman to include only basic patterns and related to aptitude as in the Dittemore study, using an experimental version of *MAP* designed by the researcher for young children.

The Miller study dealt with first grade students who had received training in usual mode and meter during kindergarten, and were assigned to experimental groups for training during first grade. Miller's study measured only tonal concepts, using major and minor for control, but added the feature of proportion of time allotted to training in less familiar modes and atonality. Training in less familiar modes was examined separately for two minor-related, two major-related, and all four less familiar modes, as well as for all modes plus nontonal training, and for exposure to only usual major and minor and nontonal categories. Again, evaluation of training was based on performance in songs.

None of the above investigations specifically verify the applicability of *ITML* norms for use in an exploratory manner to evaluate achievement of students in junior high school who have not received training specific to objectives, particularly unusual mode and meter, found in the *ITML* battery. For example, no grade has been designated as most appropriate for a particular Level of the battery. National standardization norms provide a guide only by grade ranges: for grades 4 through 6, there are norms for Levels 1, 2, and 3; for junior high school grades 7 through 9, and for senior high school grades 10 through 12, norms are offered for all Levels, 1 through 6. Further, the author states in the Manual:

> There are six Levels of the *Iowa Tests of Music Literacy* (each of which contains six subtests). The six subtests are titled the same from Level to Level because they are designed to measure parallel concepts at each Level. The content of the six subtests becomes more complex from Level 1 through Level 6. However, it is not necessary to administer the various Levels of the battery sequentially. That is, students need not take Level 1 before any other Level. Moreover, a Level may be skipped if the teacher considers a more advanced Level appropriate to students' musical understanding. The comprehensive nature of the tape-recorded directions and practice exercises makes each Level self-explanatory.[30]

It is quite conceivable that a teacher might initially administer a lower Level of *ITML* to the class. Should this Level not discriminate well because it is too easy, it is plausible that a higher Level would be administered as a consequence. Although the author states that each Level is "self-explanatory" by virture of the "comprehensive nature" of the directions and practice exercises, it is obvious that features unique to the design of the *ITML* battery and to the process of taking the subtests are paralleled within each division and throughout the six Levels of the battery. The question arises whether, in such a case, "learning effects" could accrue which might produce spuriously high scores in relation to standardization norms, based on single initial administrations of each Level of the *ITML* battery. The term "learning effects" as used in this study refers particularly to the possibility that learning could result from prior exposure to a lower Level of *ITML* in the sense that exposure to test content might constitute a program for learning sequential musical concepts embodied in higher Levels of the battery.

In the Mohatt study, it was indirectly suggested that the validity of norms for students who have not been "taught to the test" could be questioned. Further, that a first exposure to the terms and concepts involved in the subtest of *ITML* might possibly provide a learning effect. Mohatt had administered all six Levels of *ITML* to the same eighth grade students. He found that ". . . means for three of the subtests, T_2, R_1, and R_2, generally and sequentially decrease numerically, but that the means of the other three subtests, T_1, T_3, and R_3 do not." Mohatt concluded that ". . . the content validity of *ITML* can only be partially objectively substantiated."[31] Moreover, Mohatt commented regarding means for subtest R_3, "This pattern of rising scores suggests that the students might have been actually learning as they took the tests, because, from a subjective analysis, the content of the subtests becomes clearly more complex at the higher Levels."[32]

In the event that "learning effects" might be peculiar to the structure of *ITML*, either related to musical content of the subtests, or to testing procedure, such "learning effects" could impair the use of test results in that they might be misleading. Should scores reflect a short-term gain, students might be deprived of sufficient emphasis on fundamental objectives. If such learning effects were found to exist, the author would undoubtedly wish to offer supplementary norms for *ITML*. Objective evidence that having taken a given subtest before a parallel subtest at a higher Level does, or does not affect test scores would, in either case, be of practical interest to the test author and test user. Particularly, any information concerning the function of subtests within and among Levels of the battery would offer theoretical interest as an exploratory investigation related to the process of learning musical concepts.

The purpose of the study was to investigate whether "learning effects" might accrue from an initial administration of a Level of *ITML* which could increase a student's score on a higher Level of the test battery. The specific problem was to determine whether subtest scores on any Level of *ITML* higher than Level 1 could be affected by immediate prior administration of a lower Level of the battery.

Design of the Study

The investigation was designed to compare test results for the following two groups of students: those who were administered a Level of *ITML*, 2 through 6, as an initial experience with the battery comprised the "first administration groups," and those who were administered a second Level of *ITML*, 2 through 6, after experience with one of the lower Levels of the battery comprised "second administration groups." Second administration groups were further separated into comparison groups according to the previously administered lower Level.

For the six Levels of *ITML*, fifteen combinations of lower-to-higher pairs are possible. With the exception of first administrations of Level 1 (there were, of course, no second administrations of Level 1), results were utilized from both the first and second administrations of the fifteen pairs of Levels. However, Levels 4 and 5 are found as first administrations in fewer of the combinations than Levels 2 and 3, and Level 6 not at all. As shown in Table 1, six additional groups were assigned only single administrations of Levels 4, 5, and 6. In all, twenty-one groups were randomly assigned to take either single Levels or to take two Levels of *ITML*.

Table 1

Assignments of *ITML* Levels
To Twenty-One Participating Groups

First Administration Groups		Fifteen Groups: All Possible Lower-to-Higher Pairs of *ITML* Levels					Second Administration Comparison Groups
Combined Totals		1*–2	1–3	1–4	1–5	1–6	First Comparison
Level 2,	4		2–3	2–4	2–5	2–6	Second Comparison
Level 3,	3			3–4	3–5	3–6	Third Comparison
					4–5	4–6	Fourth Comparison
						5–6	Fifth Comparison
		Six Groups: Single Administrations of *ITML* Levels					
Level 4,	3	4–					
Level 5,	3	5–	5–				
Level 6,	3	6–	6–	6–			

*There was no comparison of Level 1.

Sample Population and Administration

There were three considerations in the choice of Des Moines, Iowa, for the investigation: (1) a large number of students to provide a wide range of musical achievement; (2) an established city-wide program, taught by specialists, comparable for all schools; (3) neither students nor teachers who were previously exposed to the *Iowa Tests of Music Literacy*.[33] All students regularly enrolled in eighth grade general music classes were chosen as the sample population.

To assure a representative random sample for each of the twenty-one groups required for the study, the socio-economic status of participating schools was determined. It seemed plausible that a city as large as Des Moines would exhibit socio-economic differences which might have considerable bearing on students' over-all musical achievement. According to central administrators of the school system, the twelve junior high schools in the city of Des Moines could be technically classified into three general socio-economic levels: low, average, and high.[34] It was found that four junior high schools are associated with each of the three classifications. Therefore, in an attempt to reduce possible bias due to socio-economic factors, it was decided to replicate the design in its entirety three times: once in each set of four schools, representing low, average, and high socio-economic levels. Classes were proportionally arranged among the four schools into the required twenty-one groups for each of the three replications of the study.

Administration of the study was scheduled during a four-week period set aside for city-wide testing. Music specialists agreed to complete administration of each assigned Level of *ITML* within two weeks, and to administer second Level assignments two weeks after administration of a first Level. Assignments were not announced to participating teachers in advance. Materials, including *ITML Manuals*, test tapes, and answer sheets were distributed to each teacher by the writer, just prior to administration dates, separately for first and second administrations. Standard procedures for administering the tape-recorded battery were followed as outlined in the *ITML Manual*. Each division of each Level, *Tonal Concepts* and *Rhythmic Concepts* was administered in a separate class period.

During the city-wide testing period, it was impossible to arrange for students who were absent, or excused from music classes for required comprehensive tests, to complete subtests missed from a Level of *ITML*. Therefore, it was stipulated that in order to use a student's second administration results, all twelve subtests of both assigned Levels would have to be completed. Almost one-third of the answer sheets originally distributed were incomplete and had to be eliminated from the study. The number of students from each replication of the study who completed their assigned Levels and whose test results were included in the study are reported in Table 2. In spite of the large number of incomplete tests, students from all three socio-economic districts were represented in all administration groups. Completed results of 1,349 students were included in the data. Combined totals for the five first administration groups, Levels 2 through 6, and the fifteen second administration comparison groups of the same Levels, are presented in Table 3.

Table 2

Assignment of *ITML* Levels to Classes Within and Among Schools

\multicolumn{3}{c}{Section 1 Low*}			\multicolumn{3}{c}{Section 2 Average*}			\multicolumn{3}{c}{Section 3 High*}		
First Administration Level	N	Second Administration Level	First Administration Level	N	Second Administration Level	First Administration Level	N	Second Administration Level
1	(30)	2	1	(20)	2	1	(15)	2
1	(20)	3	1	(17)	3	1	(30)	3
1	(14)	4	1	(22)	4	1	(30)	4
1	(20)	5	1	(26)	5	1	(18)	5
1	(20)	6	1	(13)	6	1	(32)	6
2	(35)	3	2	(18)	3	2	(16)	3
2	(33)	4	2	(16)	4	2	(18)	4
2	(16)	5	2	(15)	5	2	(35)	5
2	(7)	6	2	(50)	6	2	(11)	6
3	(33)	4	3	(17)	4	3	(19)	4
3	(18)	5	3	(8)	5	3	(39)	5
3	(24)	6	3	(15)	6	3	(28)	6
4	(9)	–	4	(11)	–	4	(8)	–
4	(40)	5	4	(9)	5	4	(15)	5
4	(10)	6	4	(22)	6	4	(31)	6
5	(16)	–	5	(14)	–	5	(20)	–
5	(15)	–	5	(20)	–	5	(31)	–
5	(20)	6	5	(32)	6	5	(15)	6
6	(13)	–	6	(26)	–	6	(36)	–
6	(25)	–	6	(24)	–	6	(19)	–
6	(21)	–	6	(29)	–	6	(20)	–
\multicolumn{3}{c}{Total 29 Classes}			\multicolumn{3}{c}{Total 32 Classes}			\multicolumn{3}{c}{Total 32 Classes}		

*Socio-Economic Status

Four of the twelve junior high schools of the city of Des Moines were included in each socio-economic status section. The entire study, including twenty-one administration groups, was replicated in each section of the city.

Table 3

Summary of Assignment of *ITML* Levels
Combined From Classes Within and Among Schools

First Administration	Second Administration	
Level	Level	Following Level
2 (N = 270)	2 (N = 65)	1
3 (N = 201)	3 (N = 67)	1
	3 (N = 69)	2
4 (N = 155)	4 (N = 66)	1
	4 (N = 67)	2
	4 (N = 69)	3
5 (N = 183)	5 (N = 64)	1
	5 (N = 66)	2
	5 (N = 65)	3
	5 (N = 64)	4
6 (N = 213)	6 (N = 65)	1
	6 (N = 68)	2
	6 (N = 67)	3
	6 (N = 63)	4
	6 (N = 67)	5

Analysis of the Data

For purposes of data analysis, results from the administrations of *ITML* were combined into city-wide totals. All first and single administrations from the three replications of the study were compiled for Levels 2, 3, 4, 5, and 6 for comparison with results from second administrations of the same Level. Second administration data, separated into comparison groups, 1st, 2nd, 3rd, 4th, or 5th according to the lower Level of the battery which had previously been administered, also represent the combined three replications of the study.

All answer sheets were computer-scored and raw scores were converted to standard scores.[35] Standard score means and standard deviations were derived for all administrations of the battery. Split-halves reliabilities, Spearman-Brown corrected, were computed from raw scores as were the standard errors of measurement. These data, together with relevant normative data for junior high school students, grades seven through nine, as published in the *ITML Manual*, are presented in Tables 4 through 8.[36]

Correlation coefficients were derived for students' performance on assigned pairs of lower and higher Levels of *ITML*. These correlation coefficients between parallel subtests, totals, and composite tests for the fifteen second administration comparison groups are reported in Table 9.

Table 4

Means, Standard Deviations, Reliabilities, and Standard Errors of Measurement for the *ITML* Level 2 Comparison

ITML Level 2		Tonal Concepts				Rhythmic Concepts				Composite	
		T_1	T_2	T_3	T	R_1	R_2	R_3	R	C
First Administration Level 2 (N = 270)	Mean	49.9	54.6	54.7	52.8	49.2	50.4	74.1	57.5	55.2
	S.D.	8.52	7.74	8.38	6.14	9.64	8.86	7.62	6.03	5.12
	r	.72	.70	.73	.80	.70	.74	.73	.84	.87
	S.E. Meas.	4.4	4.2	4.0	2.7	5.2	4.4	3.9	2.4	1.9
Second Administration (1)–2 (N = 65)	Mean	51.3	54.2	55.4	53.3	49.2	47.7	73.3	56.3	54.8
	S.D.	7.61	8.11	8.53	6.12	9.44	10.01	7.93	6.34	5.27
	r	.70	.73	.72	.81	.70	.80	.74	.87	.88
	S.E. Meas.	4.2	4.1	4.5	2.6	5.1	4.4	4.0	3.2	1.8
ITML* Norms Grades 7, 8, 9 Level 2	Mean	53.7	53.3	54.5	53.6	51.9	51.6	52.0	51.5	52.4
	S.D.	10.00	8.78	8.62	7.37	10.00	10.00	9.95	8.20	7.06
	r	.78	.70	.73	.83	.71	.76	.84	.86	.91
	S.E. Meas.	4.7	4.8	4.4	3.0	5.4	4.9	3.9	3.1	2.1

*Gordon, *ITML Manual*, p. 101.

Table 5

Means, Standard Deviations, Reliabilities and Standard Errors of Measurement for *ITML* Level 3 Comparisons

ITML Level 3		Tonal Concepts				Rhythmic Concepts				Composite
		T_1	T_2	T_3	T	R_1	R_2	R_3	R	C
First Administration Level 3 (N = 201)	Mean	53.3	53.6	54.9	53.5	50.7	54.9	54.1	53.2	53.3
	S.D.	7.97	9.24	10.03	7.25	8.64	8.93	9.13	6.94	5.93
	r	.71	.73	.79	.82	.72	.70	.71	.83	.84
	S.E. Meas.	4.2	4.7	4.5	3.8	4.5	4.8	4.9	2.8	2.3
First Comparison (1)–3 (N = 67)	Mean	48.9	51.1	55.7	51.6	47.2	47.3	51.9	48.4	49.9
	S.D.	8.91	11.63	9.87	7.74	9.46	11.34	9.73	7.38	7.05
	r	.70	.71	.78	.80	.70	.72	.70	.80	.82
	S.E. Meas.	4.8	5.2	4.6	3.4	5.1	5.9	5.3	3.3	2.9
Second Comparison (2)–3 (N = 69)	Mean	50.1	55.4	57.8	54.1	53.7	54.8	49.3	52.3	53.1
	S.D.	10.27	9.45	10.44	7.08	11.45	8.34	9.49	5.51	5.35
	r	.74	.70	.76	.81	.70	.70	.74	.82	.83
	S.E. Meas.	5.2	4.8	5.0	3.0	6.2	4.5	4.7	2.3	2.2
ITML* Norms Grades 7, 8, 9 Level 3	Mean	52.3	53.4	54.8	53.3	51.0	53.5	53.0	52.2	52.7
	S.D.	10.00	9.44	10.00	7.25	9.50	9.42	9.56	6.62	5.96
	r	.73	.72	.79	.82	.71	.70	.71	.81	.90
	S.E. Meas.	5.2	4.8	4.6	3.0	5.1	5.1	5.1	2.9	1.9

*Gordon, *ITML Manual*, p. 102.

Table 6

Means, Standard Deviations, Reliabilities and Standard Errors of Measurement for *ITML* Level 4 Comparisons

ITML Level 4		T_1	Tonal Concepts T_2	T_3	T	R_1	Rhythmic Concepts R_2	R_3	R	Composite C
First	Mean	47.1	45.5	57.7	49.8	45.5	43.4	47.1	45.0	47.3
Administration	S.D.	9.96	8.84	12.27	6.63	10.75	7.49	8.00	6.14	5.46
Level 4	r	.70	.70	.70	.74	.85	.74	.75	.86	.87
(N = 155)	S.E. Meas.	5.4	4.8	6.7	3.3	4.1	3.7	4.0	2.2	1.9
First	Mean	46.8	43.6	52.2	47.5	47.2	43.7	48.6	46.2	46.6
Comparison	S.D.	11.76	10.88	12.51	8.93	11.42	7.91	9.94	7.56	6.66
(1)–4	r	.70	.74	.68	.78	.86	.75	.82	.88	.88
(N = 66)	S.E. Meas.	6.4	5.5	6.9	4.1	4.2	3.7	4.2	2.6	2.2
Second	Mean	45.4	45.3	55.6	48.6	53.6	43.6	48.5	48.3	48.4
Comparison	S.D.	9.81	8.87	12.34	6.79	12.76	6.93	9.88	7.04	5.65
(2)–4	r	.69	.70	.68	.73	.78	.76	.82	.89	.89
(N = 67)	S.E. Meas.	5.5	4.8	6.8	3.5	5.9	3.3	5.2	2.3	1.8
Third	Mean	48.3	48.8	51.3	49.4	53.8	52.2	56.6	53.9	51.3
Comparison	S.D.	10.12	9.63	11.73	8.16	10.37	11.53	11.43	8.47	5.89
(3)–4	r	.71	.73	.65	.75	.80	.82	.80	.85	.90
(N = 69)	S.E. Meas.	5.4	4.9	6.9	4.0	4.6	4.8	5.1	3.2	1.8
ITML*	Mean	50.5	49.7	40.4	46.5	39.0	31.5	53.7	41.1	43.5
Norms	S.D.	10.00	9.57	6.88	4.24	10.00	10.00	9.34	8.52	5.01
Grades 7, 8, 9	r	.72	.71	.70	.80	.83	.70	.78	.84	.90
Level 4	S.E. Meas.	5.3	5.1	3.7	1.9	4.1	5.5	4.3	3.4	1.6

*Gordon, *ITML Manual*, p. 103.

Table 1

Means, Standard Deviations, Reliabilities and Standard Errors of Measurement for *ITML* Level 5 Comparisons

ITML Level 5		Tonal Concepts				Rhythmic Concepts				Composite
		T_1	T_2	T_3	T	R_1	R_2	R_3	R	C
First Administration Level 5 (N = 183)	Mean	51.5	49.9	54.2	51.5	50.3	46.7	52.0	49.3	50.3
	S.D.	10.11	10.02	9.71	7.31	10.27	8.37	8.34	6.18	6.07
	r	.70	.72	.72	.81	.82	.72	.79	.83	.87
	S.E. Meas.	5.5	5.2	5.1	3.0	4.3	4.6	3.8	2.8	2.1
First Comparison (1)–5 (N = 64)	Mean	54.1	48.4	53.5	51.7	54.7	48.8	56.5	52.9	52.3
	S.D.	9.32	7.91	8.34	5.51	10.39	9.06	9.34	6.62	5.27
	r	.72	.69	.70	.77	.79	.76	.75	.81	.85
	S.E. Meas.	4.9	4.4	4.5	2.6	4.7	4.4	4.7	2.8	2.0
Second Comparison (2)–5 (N = 66)	Mean	55.4	48.6	51.4	51.5	58.2	47.2	53.5	52.5	52.1
	S.D.	9.41	8.32	8.60	5.79	9.72	9.01	9.21	6.73	5.54
	r	.71	.69	.69	.76	.76	.75	.77	.81	.85
	S.E. Meas.	4.9	4.6	4.7	2.8	4.8	4.5	4.3	2.9	2.1
Third Comparison (3)–5 (N = 65)	Mean	55.0	51.4	53.4	53.0	56.7	51.6	58.5	55.1	54.0
	S.D.	8.77	11.07	8.62	5.98	10.24	11.81	9.54	8.41	6.64
	r	.73	.68	.70	.77	.74	.72	.73	.86	.88
	S.E. Meas.	4.5	6.1	5.2	2.8	5.2	6.2	4.9	3.1	2.3
Fourth Comparison (4)–5 (N = 64)	Mean	55.2	47.2	48.0	50.1	52.4	45.7	52.3	49.5	49.8
	S.D.	9.55	9.26	10.00	6.24	9.48	8.55	8.49	6.18	5.34
	r	.71	.70	.72	.80	.81	.71	.80	.83	.86
	S.E. Meas.	5.1	5.0	5.3	2.9	5.2	4.6	3.8	2.5	2.0
*ITML** Norms Grades 7, 8, 9 Level 5	Mean	47.5	48.0	48.0	47.7	49.6	47.8	48.5	48.5	48.1
	S.D.	9.33	9.32	9.13	6.41	9.99	8.97	9.63	6.83	5.57
	r	.71	.70	.73	.80	.80	.70	.81	.85	.91
	S.E. Meas.	5.0	5.1	4.7	2.8	4.4	4.9	4.2	2.6	1.6

*Gordon, *ITML Manual*, p. 104.

Table 8

Means, Standard Deviations, Reliabilities and Standard Errors of Measurement for *ITML* Level 6 Comparisons

ITML Level 6		T_1	T_2	T_3	T	R_1	R_2	R_3	R	Composite C
			Tonal Concepts				Rhythmic Concepts			
First Administration Level 6 (N = 213)	Mean	52.4	52.3	51.3	51.6	53.2	50.8	52.7	52.0	51.7
	S.D.	10.14	10.92	9.61	7.66	11.74	7.83	9.29	7.56	6.87
	r	.77	.72	.73	.85	.76	.75	.76	.86	.88
	S.E. Meas.	4.8	5.8	4.9	2.9	5.7	3.9	4.5	2.8	2.3
First Comparison (1)–6 (N = 65)	Mean	48.6	51.6	47.1	48.0	47.6	47.1	54.5	49.4	49.1
	S.D.	9.13	7.64	8.44	4.52	10.43	6.22	8.59	5.94	4.23
	r	.80	.75	.71	.81	.80	.70	.73	.82	.84
	S.E. Meas.	4.1	3.8	4.5	1.9	4.6	3.4	4.4	2.5	1.6
Second Comparison (2)–6	Mean	46.2	48.8	47.4	47.4	51.7	48.0	55.1	51.4	49.5
	S.D.	10.06	10.45	9.01	6.67	11.72	8.80	9.18	6.99	5.70
	r	.79	.78	.72	.82	.78	.73	.70	.84	.85

Table 8 (continued)

(N = 68)	S.E. Meas.	4.6	4.9	4.7	2.8	5.5	4.6	5.0	2.8	2.2
Third Comparison (3)–6	Mean	48.3	51.7	47.6	48.8	45.4	47.0	55.7	49.1	49.0
	S.D.	9.45	10.09	10.84	7.03	9.90	8.43	8.48	5.50	5.06
	r	.80	.75	.74	.84	.79	.72	.73	.82	.85
(N = 67)	S.E. Meas.	4.2	5.0	5.5	2.8	4.5	4.5	4.4	2.3	1.9
Fourth Comparison (4)–6	Mean	49.2	51.7	47.4	49.1	49.7	47.9	55.2	50.6	49.9
	S.D.	9.94	9.93	6.97	6.01	9.82	6.64	8.39	5.34	4.53
	r	.82	.78	.70	.83	.86	.70	.73	.88	.89
(N = 63)	S.E. Meas.	4.2	4.6	3.8	2.4	3.7	3.6	4.3	1.8	1.5
Fifth Comparison (5)–6	Mean	49.5	53.5	47.7	49.7	50.8	47.6	55.3	50.9	50.4
	S.D.	8.76	10.45	9.56	7.52	10.79	8.44	9.63	7.37	6.65
	r	.81	.71	.73	.84	.85	.72	.71	.87	.88
(N = 67)	S.E. Meas.	3.7	5,6	4.9	3.0	4.1	4.4	5.2	2.6	2.2
ITML* Norms Grades 7, 8, 9 Level 6	Mean	49.6	49.4	48.5	49.0	45.3	53.8	52.0	50.4	49.6
	S.D.	10.00	9.78	9.46	7.05	10.00	10.00	8.86	7.79	4.98
	r	.80	.70	.71	.84	.82	.72	.75	.85	.90
	S.E. Meas.	4.5	5.3	5.1	2.8	4.2	5.3	4.4	3.0	1.5

*Gordon, *ITML Manual*, p. 105.

Table 9

Correlation Coefficients Between Parallel
Subtests, Totals, and Composite Scores
Derived for Fifteen Second Administration
Pairs of Lower-to-Higher Levels of *ITML*

ITML Levels	T_1	T_2	T_3	T	R_1	R_2	R_3	R	C
1 and 2	32*	62	70	77	17	55	42	54	76
1 and 3	37	72	74	71	11	37	56	62	78
2 and 3	00	44	56	43	24	19	47	51	61
1 and 4	04	70	−12	52	37	40	49	66	75
2 and 4	−21	44	−22	11	21	24	51	40	51
3 and 4	−12	37	−15	−32	14	71	72	82	63
1 and 5	39	−10	56	45	−10	22	40	46	61
2 and 5	50	23	55	58	28	29	43	50	51
3 and 5	23	45	69	81	56	70	72	76	80
4 and 5	16	48	47	49	43	49	58	43	65
1 and 6	51	00	−14	39	21	35	76	50	48
2 and 6	37	11	30	21	32	40	53	47	46
3 and 6	17	21	26	36	16	29	59	41	49
4 and 6	28	61	61	35	60	24	71	68	82
5 and 6	57	31	47	70	81	46	54	73	80

*For ease in reading, decimals do not precede coefficients.

Further, for only the higher Levels of the pairs — the fifteen second administration comparisons of Levels 2, 3, 4, 5, and 6 — inter-correlation coefficients were derived among subtests of each division, *Tonal Concepts* and *Rhythmic Concepts*. These intercorrelation coefficients are presented in Table 10.

Standard score frequency distributions derived for the five first and fifteen second administrations of Levels 2 through 6 were plotted, graphically smoothed, and converted to percentile ranks for all nine scores yielded by *ITML*. Thirteen percentile ranks were selected from these distributions for comparisons: 1, 5, 10, 15, 25, 40, 50, 60, 75, 85, 90, 95, and 99. Comparisons were based on a generalized error of measurement, arbitrarily set by the writer. Because standard errors of measurement derived for subtests of the battery, although varied, were found to be near or in excess of 4 standard score points, the amount was adopted as a difference "of consequence" to be critically examined. In Table 11, those second administration distributions with discrepancies of 4 or more standard score points are reported by subtest and compared with first administration distributions and with the appropriate standard score-percentile rank equivalents derived from the national standardization of *ITML Manual* (Tables of Percentile Norms, pp. 121–151). All subtest comparisons of the study are summarized in Table 12 to indicate the differences which could be considered the effect on higher Levels of *ITML*, 2 through 6, of experience with each lower Level of the battery, 1 through 5. Corresponding standard score distributions reported by Levels for all of the comparisons of the study are included in the Appendix.

Table 10

Intercorrelations Among Subtests within
Tonal and Rhythmic Divisions for Higher
Levels of Fifteen Second Administration Groups

ITML Level	Comparison Group	Tonal Concepts			Rhythmic Concepts		
		T_1 T_2	T_2 T_3	T_3	R_1 R_2	R_2 R_3	R_3
2	(1)	60	53	70	37	45	66
3	(1)	30	19	60	25	25	32
3	(2)	05	23	44	06	−22	10
4	(1)	62	−03	−08	39	34	47
4	(2)	29	01	−13	20	32	13
4	(3)	37	−08	−13	24	50	37
5	(1)	−01	17	24	11	19	45
5	(2)	13	14	22	38	11	36
5	(3)	−23	−07	51	45	31	58
5	(4)	09	01	06	22	27	42
6	(1)	22	−34	−02	24	17	34
6	(2)	27	00	40	22	21	41
6	(3)	41	06	22	17	−14	22
6	(4)	38	−16	23	18	−05	27
6	(5)	40	24	51	32	35	40

For ease in reading, decimals do not precede coefficients.

Table 11

Standard Score-Percentile Rank Equivalents For First and Second Administration Distributions Of *ITML* Subtests in which Differences of Consequence Were Observed with the Corresponding Standard Scores From the *ITML* Standardization Data Grade Range 7 through 9

Tonal *Aural Perception*

PR	T_1 5+ (1)–5++		T_1 5 (2)–5		T_1 5 (3)–5		T_1 5 (4)–5		T_1 6 (2)–6		ITML Level 5	ITML Level 6
99	77+ *77	++77	77	77 75	77	77 77	77	77 71	70 70	70	70	70
95	71	72	71	71	71	72	71	68	66	65	66	67
90	65	68	65	67	65	67	65	65	62	60	61	63
85	60	64	60	63	60	63	60	62	59	56	58	60
75	56	60	56	60	56	60	56	59	56	52	53	55
60	53	56	53	57	53	57	53	57	54	49	49	51
50	50	53	50	54	50	54	50	55	52	46	47	49
40	47	50	47	51	47	51	47	53	49	43	45	46
25	44	46	44	47	44	48	44	50	46	40	41	42
15	41	42	41	43	41	45	41	46	42	37	37	39
10	38	38	38	39	38	42	38	41	38	33	35	37
5	34	33	34	35	34	38	34	36	33	29	30	33
1	30	28	30	30	30	34	30	30	27	25	26	29

*ITML Ceiling Score for Subtest of Stated Level (from norms Grade Range 10–12).
+First Administration distribution 5. For example, First Administration of Level 5.
++Second Administration distribution (1)–5. For example, Second Administration of Level 5 following Level 1.

Table 11. (continued)

Tonal *Reading Recognition*

PR	T_2 4+ ++(1)–4		T_2 5 (4)–5		T_2 6 (2)–6		ITML Level 4	5	6
99	65+ ++67	*75	77	80 69	76	79 75	69	69	71
95	61	62	71	64	70	69	65	65	67
90	57	57	65	59	65	64	62	60	62
85	53	52	60	55	61	59	60	57	59
75	50	48	55	51	58	55	56	54	55
60	47	44	51	48	55	51	52	50	51
50	45	42	48	45	52	48	50	48	49
40	42	39	46	43	49	46	48	46	46
25	39	36	43	41	46	43	43	41	42
15	36	33	39	38	42	40	40	37	38
10	34	30	35	35	37	36	38	35	36
5	31	27	30	31	32	31	33	32	33
1	27	23	25	27	26	26	29	28	29

+First Administration distribution 4. For example, First Administration of Level 4.
++Second Administration distribution (1)–4. For example, Second Administration of Level 4 following Level 1.
*ITML Ceiling Score.

Table 11 (continued)

Tonal *Notational Understanding*

PR	T_3 4+	(3)–4++	T_3 5	(4)–5	T_3 6	(4)–6	ITML Level 4	5	6
99	80+ *80	80++	75	75 67	74	80 68	70	67	69
95	75	74	70	63	69	64	66	63	65
90	71	69	66	59	64	60	61	60	60
85	67	64	62	55	60	57	56	57	58
75	64	60	59	52	57	54	49	54	54
60	61	56	56	49	54	51	43	50	51
50	58	52	53	47	52	48	40	48	49
40	55	48	51	45	50	46	38	45	46
25	51	44	48	42	47	44	35	40	42
15	46	39	45	39	43	41	32	37	39
10	40	34	41	35	39	38	30	35	37
5	33	28	37	30	34	35	25	32	32
1	25	22	32	25	29	32	21	28	28

+First Administration distribution 4. For example, First Administration of Level 4.
++Second Administration distribution (3)–4. For example, Second Administration of Level 4 following Level 3.
*ITML Ceiling Score.

Table 11 (continued)

Rhythmic Aural Perception

PR	R_1 3+ (1)–3++		R_1 4 (2)–4		R_1 4 (3)–4		R_1 5 (2)–5		R_1 5 (3)–5		R_1 6 (3)–6		ITML Level 3	ITML Level 4	ITML Level 5	ITML Level 6
99	74+ ++70	*80	71	73 73	71	73 73	73	73 73	73	73 73	70	70 68	73	–	68	–
95	69	66	65	69	65	69	67	71	67	69	66	63	69	–	65	68
90	64	62	59	65	59	65	62	69	62	66	62	58	64	68	62	63
85	60	58	54	62	54	62	58	67	58	63	58	54	61	63	60	59
75	56	54	50	59	50	59	54	64	54	61	55	50	56	53	56	54
60	52	50	47	56	47	56	51	61	51	59	53	47	53	42	52	48
50	49	47	45	53	45	53	49	58	49	57	51	45	51	39	50	45
40	46	44	43	50	43	50	47	55	47	55	48	43	49	37	48	42
25	42	40	41	46	41	46	45	52	45	53	45	41	44	33	43	37
15	38	37	38	41	38	42	43	49	43	50	42	38	41	29	40	32
10	34	34	34	35	34	37	40	45	40	46	38	35	39	28	37	29
5	30	31	29	27	29	31	36	41	36	42	33	32	34	24	32	25
1	25	27	23	20	23	25	31	36	31	37	27	28	30	20	28	21

+First Administration distribution 3. For example, First Administration of Level 3.
++Second Administration distribution (1)–3. For example, Second Administration of Level 3 following Level 1.
*ITML Ceiling Score.

Table 11 (continued)

Rhythmic *Reading Recognition*

PR	R₂ 3+ (1)–3++		R₂ 4 (3)–4		R₂ 5 (3)–5		R₂ 5 (4)–5		R₂ 6 (3)–6		R₂ 6 (5)–6		ITML Level			
													3	4	5	6
99	75+ ++75	*80	64	77 72	70	77 71	70	77 68	68	79 66	68	79 69	72	–	71	–
95	72	70	58	66	65	67	65	62	64	62	64	65	68	–	67	76
90	70	65	53	61	60	63	60	57	61	58	61	60	60	70	62	71
85	68	60	49	57	56	60	56	52	58	55	58	56	63	65	58	67
75	65	55	46	54	52	57	52	48	55	52	55	52	59	55	54	62
60	60	50	44	52	48	54	48	45	52	49	52	49	56	40	50	56
50	56	46	43	51	45	52	45	43	50	46	50	46	54	31	48	54
40	52	43	41	49	43	50	43	42	48	44	48	44	52	28	45	50
25	48	40	38	46	41	47	41	41	46	42	46	41	47	25	41	44
15	43	36	35	42	38	44	38	39	43	38	43	38	42	23	38	37
10	38	32	32	37	35	40	35	37	39	34	39	35	40	22	35	32
5	33	28	29	31	31	36	31	34	34	30	34	32	35	21	30	27
1	28	24	25	25	27	31	27	30	28	25	28	28	31	20	26	23

+First Administration distribution 3. For example, First Administration of Level 3.
++Second Administration distribution (1)–3. For example, Second Administration of Level 3 following Level 1.
*ITML Ceiling Score.

Table 11 (continued)

Rhythmic *Notational Understanding*

PR	R_3 3+ (1)–3++		R_3 3 (2)–3		R_3 4 (3)–4		R_3 5 (1)–5		R_3 5 (3)–5		R_3 5 (4)–5		ITML Level 3	4	5
99	80+ ++78	*80	80	80 75	65	80 75	80	80 80	80	80 80	80	80 74	75	77	70
95	75	73	75	70	61	71	73	75	73	75	73	69	70	73	66
90	70	68	70	65	57	67	67	70	67	70	67	64	66	68	61
85	66	64	66	61	54	64	62	65	62	66	62	60	62	63	58
75	62	60	62	57	52	61	58	61	58	63	58	57	58	59	54
60	58	56	58	53	50	58	55	58	55	60	55	54	55	56	50
50	55	52	55	50	48	55	52	56	52	57	52	52	53	54	48
40	52	49	52	47	46	52	49	52	49	54	49	50	51	52	46
25	49	46	49	44	44	48	46	48	46	50	46	47	46	48	42
15	46	43	46	41	41	44	43	43	43	46	43	43	43	45	38
10	43	39	43	38	37	39	39	38	39	41	39	38	41	43	36
5	39	35	39	34	33	33	35	33	35	36	35	33	36	39	31
1	35	31	35	30	28	26	30	28	30	30	30	27	32	35	27

+First Administration distribution 3. For example, First Administration of Level 3.
++Second Administration distribution (1)–3. For example, Second Administration of Level 3 following Level 1.
*ITML Ceiling Score.

Table 12

Summary of Differences in Standard Score Points Between First and Second Administrations at Thirteen Selected Percentile Ranks Arranged According to High, Average, and Low Achievement

Following Level 1		T_1	T_2	T_3	R_1	R_2	R_3
2	H*	1	−2, −1	1	S, −1	−2, −1	S
	A	2	−1	1	S	−3, −2	−1
	L	1	S, −1	1, S	−1	−2, −3	S
3	H	−2	−1, S, 1	−1, S	*−2, −3, −4	*−8, −5, −2	−2
	A	−1, −2	S, −1, −2	−1	−2	*−8, −9, −10	−3, −2
	L	−2, −1, S	1, S	−1	1, S	*−4, −5, −6, −7	*−4
4	H	S, 1, 2	−1, S, 1, 2	−1, S	2	−1	2
	A	S	−3, −2	−3, −2	1, 2	−1	1
	L	−3, −2, −1, S	*−4, −3	−3	−2, −1, S	−1	−1, S, 1
5	H	*4, 3, 1, S	S, −1, −2	S, −1, −2	S	2, 1, S	3, 2, S
	A	*2, 3, 4	S	S	1, 2, 1	1, 2, 3	*2, 3, 4, 3
	L	−2, −1, S, 1	2, 1, S	1, S	S	−2, −1, S	−2, −1, S
6	H	−2, −1	−2	−3	S	−3	1, S, −2
	A	−2	−2	−3	−3, −2, 1	−3	2
	L	−2	3, 1, S, −1	S, −1, −2	2, S, −2, −3	2, S, −1, −2	2

*High = 85, 90, 95, 99 PR
Average = 25, 40, 50, 60, 75 PR
Low = 1, 5, 10, 15 PR

All figures represent the difference between the standard score for the Second Administration group as compared to that of the First Administration group at comparable percentile ranks.
S indicates same; differences are increased standard scores except where negative sign is used.

[134]

Table 12 (continued)

Following Level 2		T_1	T_2	T_3	R_1	R_2	R_3
3	H*	S,1,2	1	1,2	2	−1	*−5
	A	−1	1	1	2	−1,−2,−1	*−5
	L	−2,−1	1	2,1	−2,−1,1,2	−1	*−5
4	H	−2	−1	−1,S	*8,6,4,2	−1	2,3
	A	−2	−1	−1	*5,7,8,9	1,S,−1	S,1
	L	−2	−1	−1	−3,−2,1,3	2,1	S
5	H	3,2,S,−2	S,−1,−2	−2	*9,8,5,2	S	S
	A	*3,4	−2,−1,S	−3,−2	*7,8,9,10	S	S,1,S
	L	S,1,2	2,1,S,−1	S,−1,−2,−3	*5,6	S	−1
6	H	−3,−2,−1,S	−2,−1	−2	1,S	−2,−1,S	2,1,−1,−2
	A	*−6,−5,−4	*−3,−4,−3	−3	1	−3,−2	1,2,3
	L	*−2,−4,−5	S,−1,−2	−1,−2,−3	S	−3	−3,−3,−2,S

*High = 85, 90, 95, 99 PR
Average = 25, 40, 50, 60, 75 PR
Low = 1, 5, 10, 15 PR

All figures represent the difference between the standard score for the Second Administration Group as compared to that of the First Administration Group at comparable percentile ranks.
S indicates same; differences are increased standard scores except where negative sign is used.

Table 12 (continued)

Following Level 3		T_1	T_2	T_3	R_1	R_2	R_3
4	H*	1,S	2,1,S	−3,−2,−1,S	*8,6,4,2	*8	*10
	A	1	2	*−7,−6,−5,−4	*5,7,8,9	*8	*4,6,7,8,9
	L	1	2	*−3,−5,−6,−7	*2,3,4	*S,2,5,7	−2,S,2,3
5	H	3,2,1,S	1,S,−1	−2	*5,4,2,S	*4,3,2	*4,3,2,S
	A	*4	2	1,2,S,−1,−2	*8,7	*6,7,6,5	*4,5
	L	*4	−1,S,1,2	3,2	*6,7	*4,5,6	S,1,2,3
6	H	S,−1	S,−2	−3	*−4,−4,−3,−2	−3,−2	2,1,−1,−2
	A	−2,−1,S	−2,−1	*−4,−3	*−4,−5,−6,−5	*−4,−3	2,3
	L	−2	−2	*−4	*1,−1,−3,−4	*−3,−4,−5	1,2

*High = 85, 90, 95, 99 PR
Average = 25, 40, 50, 60, 75 PR
Low = 1, 5, 10, 15 PR

All figures represent the difference between the standard score for the Second Administration Group as compared to that of the First Administration Group at comparable percentile ranks.
S indicates same; differences are increased standard scores except where negative sign is used.

Table 12 (continued)

		T_1	T_2	T_3	R_1	R_2	R_3
Following Level 4							
5	H	*2,S,−3,−6	*−5,−6,−7,−8	*−7,−8	1	*−4,−3,−2	*−2,−3,−4,−6
	A	*6,7,5,4,3	*−2,−3,−4	*−6,−7	2,1	*S,−1,−2,−3,−4	1,S,−1
	L	*S,2,3,5	2,1,S,−1	*−7,−6	3,2	3,2,1	−3,−2,−1,S
6	H	−1,−2	−2	*−3,−4,−5,−6	−1,−2,−3	−3	1,S,−1,−2
	A	−3,−2,−1	−2,−3	*−3,−4,−3	S,−1	−3	1,2,3,2
	L	−2	−2	3,1,−1,−2	1,S	2,S,−2,−3	1,S,1
Following Level 5							
6	H	−2,−1,S	−1,S	−3,−2,−1,1	S	−2,−1,1	1,S,−1
	A	−1,−2,−3,−2	−1	−2,−3	S	*−5,−4,−3	S,1,2,1
	L	2,1,S	−1	1,S,−1	1,S	*S,−2,−4,−5	−1,−2

*High = 85, 90, 95, 99 PR
Average = 25, 40, 50, 60, 75 PR
Low = 1, 5, 10, 15 PR

All figures represent the difference between the standard score for the Second Administration Group as compared to that of the First Administration Group at comparable percentile ranks.
S indicates same; differences are increased standard scores except where negative sign is used.

Summary of Results and Conclusions

Criteria established for this study to support a "learning effect," improvement of +4 standard score points, was met at some range of achievement in score distributions of thirteen out of ninety subtest comparisons. In an additional eighteen subtests, the criterion effect was met at some range of achievement, but differences found in standard score-percentile rank equivalents for second administration groups were negative. The proportion of subtests where learning effects were found was not great enough, nor systematic enough, to suggest feasibility of a second set of norms.

Therefore, until further information is available, it is recommended that for students without previous training toward objectives of the given Levels, the following subtests should not be administered in an exploratory fashion immediately after corresponding subtests of the indicated lower Levels, because there is reason to believe that resultant scores may be spuriously high:

T_1: Tonal *Aural Perception*, Level 5 after Levels 1, 2, 3, and 4.

R_1: Rhythmic *Aural Perception*, Levels 4 and 5, after Levels 2 and 3.

R_2: Rhythmic *Reading Recognition*, Levels 4 and 5 after Level 3.

R_3: Rhythmic *Notational Understanding*, Levels 4 and 5 after Level 3, and Level 5 after Level 1.

In addition, because observed negative effects give reason to expect that resultant scores may be spuriously low, the following subtests should not be administered immediately after corresponding subtests of the indicated lower Levels:

T_1: Tonal *Aural Perception*, Level 5 after Level 4; and Level 6 after Level 2.

T_2: Tonal *Reading Recognition*, Level 4 after Level 1; Level 5 after Level 4; and Level 6 after Level 2.

T_3: Tonal *Notational Understanding*, Levels 4 and 6 after Level 3; and Levels 5 and 6 after Level 4.

R_1: Rhythmic *Aural Perception*, Level 3 after Level 1; and Level 6 after Level 3.

R_2: Rhythmic *Reading Recognition*, Level 3 after Level 1; Level 5 after Level 4; and Level 6 after Levels 3 and 5.

R_3: Rhythmic *Notational Understanding*, Level 3 after Levels 1 and 2; and Level 5 after Level 4.

Conclusions

The practical concern of the study had arisen from curricular needs of music education to be observed most acutely in a terminal class in General Music, frequently in junior high school. In this regard, it is suggested that the study be replicated and the design incorporate varying periods of time, to determine whether observed effects would persist. In addition, it is suggested that measures of musical aptitude, verbal intelligence, and mathematical intelligence be correlated with results for *ITML* subtests of aural and visual achievement.

Interpretation of the Data

The question whether norms derived from single administrations of Levels of the battery of musical achievement tests, the *Iowa Tests of Music Literacy*, would apply to the exploratory use of more than one Level of the battery in close succession, or whether learning effects would accrue which might impair the use of norms to evaluate results from second administrations, arose from the unique structure of *ITML* and the generally subjective nature of music curricula. Some results, at first surprising and seemingly inconsistent, provided challenging problems related to the process of learning music.

It occurred to the writer that experience with test items in the *ITML* battery might be conducive to learning in that the sequence of *Tonal Concepts* and *Rhythmic Concepts* have been structured to measure development in music literacy in relation to a sense of tonality and a sense of rhythm. Interpretation of the data has been expanded to include a critical examination of aspects unique to the battery: perception of tone and of rhythm in terms of a vocabulary of patterns; sequential difficulty of the vocabulary of tone patterns and rhythm patterns; and, identification of categories of mode and meter.

With interpretations evolved a term, "aural imagery." Aural imagery signifies to the writer ability to recognize or supply tonal or rhythmic organization of a pattern in relation to resting tone or tempo beats. Aural imagery indicates, therefore, the ability to image the *musical meaning* of sound patterns, not in relation to evoked visual images, or in an affective sense, but in relation to a sense of tonality and a sense of rhythm. The meaning of a musical pattern implies the usefulness of a pattern for transfer to symbolic notation or for creative use. It follows that relative imagery inherent within a pattern would be in terms of available information for identification of mode or meter.

In the quotation from the *ITML Manual* tested in this study, Gordon stated that it is not necessary to take Level 1 before any other Level of the battery. Presumably this statement arises from the *fundamental* nature of basic tonal and rhythmic concepts incorporated in test items of Level 1 in their most simple form. Recognition of and discrimination between major or minor mode and duple or triple meter is presented by the test author as fundamental to identification by comparison or contrast of more advanced and complex examples of mode or meter comprised in the sequence of higher Levels of the battery. As can be seen in Table 12, the author's statement is not entirely in accord with the findings of this study. Of fifteen comparisons of subtests in the *Tonal Concepts* division, two instances of *differences of consequence were found:* for students of above average achievement a positive effect in the first comparison of Level 5, T_1, and at the lowest percentile rank, a negative effect in the first comparison of Level 4, T_2; both in the amount of 4 standard score points. Among the fifteen comparisons in the *Rhythmic Concepts* division, differences in the amount of 4 standard score points were observed as a positive effect for students at the median for subtest R_3, in the first comparison of Level 5; and as negative effects in the first comparison of Level 3, on subtest R_1, at the highest percentile rank; and on subtest R_3, at the lowest percentile rank. However, also in the first comparison of Level 3, more severe negative effects, as great in magnitude as -10 standard score points, were observed from the lowest rank to the range of high achievement. Although in the main, the test author's statement is corroborated for conditions of this study, it is possible that *it* might not apply to students in lower grades, particularly because Level 3 is normed for students of grade range 4 through 6.

Negative Differences

A difference "of consequence" was found in relatively few comparisons. What is immediately evident in Table 12 is that there were more instances of negative than of positive differences large enough to warrant attention. It could be considered that, by chance, perhaps due to loss of incomplete test results, some comparison groups may not have been as capable as their counterparts in the larger first administration groups. Personality factors, such as frustration or lack of motivation, could also be used to account for negative differences demonstrated in some comparisons.

In a study of the "In-Doubt-Response"[37] using standard and experimental forms of *ITML*, Foss alternated the order of presentation among his subjects. In all cases, higher validity coefficients were achieved for first administrations of selected Levels, whether standard or experimental. He reported, "A possible reason for this result is that students might not have sustained their interest when taking the tests the second time."[38] Students in the Foss study were taking parallel forms of the same Levels, and may not have sustained interest. Comparison of test content with observed distributions, suggests that interpretation specific to results found for this study would be more appropriate.

Negative differences do not seem to be systematic, but to reflect different demands of the subtests. In some comparisons, subtests may have seemed more difficult to students in the second administration group by contrast with their previous experience. For example, perhaps because they were too "easy" with the one exception previously mentioned, literacy subtests in Level 1 did not provide a "learning situation." Negative differences such as Tonal *Reading*

Recognition, for students of lowest achievement in the first comparison of Level 4 and subtests in the *Rhythmic Concepts* division for the first comparison group of Level 3 are examples. In particular, subtest R_3 in the second comparison of Level 3 seems to represent such a contrast. Subtest R_3, Level 2, was found to be extremely easy for Des Moines students in comparison with national norms. Yet, for students in the second comparison group of Level 3, the entire distribution was -5 standard score points below that of students who took Level 3 as an initial experience with the battery.

In other cases, unfamiliarity with terms, procedures, or concepts, shared by both administration groups, seems to have been exacerbated for students in second administration groups. Uncertainty in responding to subtest items encountered in both their first and second assigned Levels of *ITML*, may have been confounded by the brief span of two weeks between administrations of the two Levels. The above reasoning seems particularly applicable to negative differences found for literacy subtests in the fourth comparison of Level 5, T_2 and T_3, and subtest T_3 in the fourth comparison of Level 6, as well. Literacy skills required in subtest T_2 include for Level 4 recognition of nontonal patterns, many key signatures and all accidentals. Although heard in major and minor, items for Level 5 are written with two voice-parts and many key signatures. In the fourth comparison of subtest T_3, Level 6, advanced literacy skills included use of the bass clef in Level 4. Negative correlations found on subtest T_3 for all Level 4 comparison groups are presumably due to unfamiliarity with use of the bass clef. Further, test items for T_3 in Level 6 are comprised of nontonal patterns written with all accidentals in two voice-parts. Similarly, negative differences were observed in isolated rhythmic subtests in comparison groups assigned higher Level pairs.

Thus, inadequacy to cope with visual skills demanded in higher Level subtests is reflected in negative results for those students who, within a brief span of time, encountered two sets of unfamiliar requirements in advanced subtests of literacy achievement. Certainly, as shown in Table 10, intercorrelation coefficients differ among subtests of higher Levels administered to separate comparison groups. A factor of expectancy could be reflected in the extent of negative differences found for some second administration groups, initiated by the degree of difficulty encountered in test items of the lower Level previously experienced. It seems most likely that negative effects for second administration groups emphasize the lack of something basic to achievement in music.

Tonal Concepts

Positive differences "of consequence" among comparisons in the *Tonal Concepts* division of the battery were found only for the *Aural Perception* subtest, T_1, in Level 5. Students from second administration groups within ranges of low, average, or above-average achievement attained higher scores on subtest T_1 than students of comparable achievement from the first administration group in all four comparisons of Level 5. The consistent improvement of a score distribution over all comparisons of a Level was not observed for any other subtest in the battery.

Scores for the first three comparison groups were improved by +4 standard score points, the amount set by this writer to warrant interpretation: following Level 1 at the 75th and 85th percentiles; after experience with Level 2, from the 40th through the 75th percentiles; and after experience with Level 3, throughout the entire low and average ranges of achievement. However, for students in the fourth comparison group, although standard scores were higher from the 15th through the 60th percentiles, increasing to +7 at the 40th percentile, differences decreased to −6 at the 99th percentile. This decrease in standard score-percentile rank equivalents is especially notable because students in the first and third comparison groups attained the ceiling of the test, as did the first administration group.

Tonal *Aural Perception* subtests of *ITML* have been designed to measure development of skills requisite to aural identification of mode. Gordon states, ". . . the musical mind aurally perceives sound and then conceptually organizes that sound into tonal meaning according to implications of the tonality (the resting tone and mode and not necessarily the key) of the music."[39] Perception of mode then, requires awareness of a resting tone; that awareness to be implied in some manner. Ethnomusicologists and historians present evidence for diatonic and for harmonic function in identification of a tonic or resting tone. What is cultural and what is natural to human perception of mode has never been specifically identified.

In interpreting results of the study, this writer entertains the hypothesis that musical tones can be related to tonality when at least three dimensions are perceived, or "aurally imaged"; and immediate "surface level" of perception — a pattern of tones; a next-deeper level of perception — perhaps only a dominant-to-tonic relationship — possibly a harmonic function, which could be implied as in unison melody; and the deepest level, the fundamental reference for tonal relationships — the resting tone. It should follow that interaction of harmonic implications and resting tone establish mode, but diatonic characteristics also apply — probably, learned associations.

The boundaries of a mode in Western culture are a tonic and its octave. The number, size, and disposition of "steps" between the limits of an octave constitute a mode — whether objective "by nature," culturally accepted, or arbitrarily designed. Interestingly, relative pitches tempered to permit free interchange in modulations do not affect the dominant. Recognition of a tendency toward a tonic could be more or less a matter of learning, depending on whether the dominant in relation to a tonic is necessary to establish a resting tone, whether further harmonic implications provide this tendency, or whether smaller intervals, for example, halfsteps, promote the suggestion of tonic resting tone. As observed from at least Baroque times, less familiar modes also assume major or minor tonality, relative to tonic harmony. Thus, familiarity with modal characteristics (like the variations of "natural minor") would be considered functions of achievement.

The sequence of *Tonal Concepts* in successive Levels of *ITML* incorporates patterns, modes, categories, and key relationships in unison, two-voice counterpoint, and three-part harmony — represented aurally in subtest T_1. Specific aural skills are rarely stated as sequential tonal objectives in General Music classes. Rather, listening skills are generally related to form, historic style, and instrumentation in pursuit of music appreciation.[40] Emphasis can be expected on visual skills related to reading music for performance. It is reasonable to assume that demands of subtest items in T_1 provided a new experience for subjects in the study according to the Level which they experienced initially.

Identical response options, major and minor, were found in lower and higher Levels by first and second comparison groups of Level 5. Items for subtest T_1, Level 1, are comprised of tone patterns classified as "basic." Simple in difficulty, basic patterns are designed of tones from tonic or dominant triads with passing tones, beginning or ending on the tonic. It should be noted that the test author utilizes the harmonic form of minor. Because half-step leading tones are similar, basic patterns stress only differences between the sounds of major and minor tonic triads. In Level 2 some tone patterns are complex; that is, the tones are more remote harmonically or do not necessarily begin or end on the tonic. Similarly, some tone patterns are complex in Level 5 test items. In Levels 1 and 2 major items are heard in C and minor items are heard in A, but test items are heard in a variety of keys in Level 5 with concomitant changes of tonic pitch.

For their initial experience with *ITML*, students in third and fourth comparison groups found response options unique to *ITML*: "usual" and "unusual." The terms, presented in practice exercises preceding subtests, group either major or minor tone patterns into the category "usual" in the sense of familiar. The "unusual" category signifies less familiar. Unusual test items in Level 3 contain tone patterns in some less familiar mode such as Dorian or Phrygian; in Level 4, unusual test items are nontonal. In both Levels 3 and 4, tone patterns in the usual category may be complex in difficulty, but unusual items are classified as basic, denoting simple. Also, test items in Levels 3 and 4 are heard in several keys as are those of Level 5.

The most obvious feature of interest in this finding of improved scores is related to test items in Level 5. Options for Level 5, T_1, are again either major or minor. Test items comprised of tone patterns which may be complex are presented contrapuntally in two voice-parts; in the first voice-part, items are comprised of seven tones, but second voice-parts incorporating some root tones of harmonic progressions vary from two to seven tones. Simultaneous tones are, of course, perceptible as harmonic dyads which conceivably might enhance identification of mode.

An hypothesis which might be acceptable to explain this somewhat troublesome finding, but which certainly requires considerable research, is that aural recognition of basic major and minor tone patterns is a function of tonal aptitude. That is, students may acquire recognition of major and minor tonality with little effort, merely through sufficient exposure, when patterns are limited to "basic" patterns. This is because basic patterns are "preorganized," perceived, according to tonal aptitude, obviously. Thus basic patterns demand little attention. Because only recognition is required, a resting tone need not be supplied. Complex problems of discrimination, however, require the use of aural imagery and thus demand considerable attention. Therefore, students did not benefit as noticeably from taking Level 1, but did demonstrate benefit from attention necessary to discern mode of patterns in Level 2. This suggests not only the importance of informal learning, either to recognize or to acquire basic relationships, but also limitations of informal learning.

As shown in Table 9, comparatively high correlation coefficients were observed between parallel subtests of Tonal *Aural Perception*, T_1, for the first three comparison groups of Level 5, reflecting familiarity with major and minor modes and a recognition of "usual" resting tones. The highest correlation, .50, between Levels 2 and 5, corroborates the test author's identification of complexity in tone patterns for these two Levels.

The nature of test items in Level 5, although complex, may have offered more positive identification of options for students, and therefore, could have seemed easier than items in Level 2. Because second voice-parts, used sparsely in test items for Level 5, may have served to heighten the impression of resting tones or dominant-to-tonic characteristics of major or harmonic minor modes, a student would then be relieved of the demand to supply an imperceptible resting tone through aural imagery.

Among the comparisons of Level 5, that following Level 4 is a compressed distribution with its bulk of scores observed as a low mode at the 40th percentile. This finding could suggest, by chance, a group inferior in achievement. A rather low correlation, .16, was derived between results for Levels 4 and 5, T_1, indicative of the considerable differences in aural perception of test items in categories assigned to the two Levels. Although it is difficult to attribute the lack of extremes in achievement found in the distribution of T_1 for the Level 5 fourth comparison group to unfamiliarity with nontonal patterns, organization of tonal perception merits further consideration. The possibility of inherent complexity in perception of nontonal patterns as opposed to patterns with objective tonality, major, minor, or even modal, is an interesting speculation.

Related to this question are results from three experimental investigations which involved individual performance after training. Especially pertinent to learning effects on Level 5, T_1, is Dittemore's conclusion, based on one week's training, that two-part music was performed well by students of average or high aptitude from grades three to six, and three part music only by high aptitude students in grade five and average and high aptitude students in grade six. Although the same criterion songs chosen from a grade five basic series text were used to represent selected musical concepts for all grade levels, other factors contributing to difficulty could not be isolated. A nonetheless surprising result of Dittemore's findings in tonal measures was that first grade children scored well only on the minor song. The minor song used was in natural minor, or aeolian mode — considered to be a less familiar form of minor in our culture. Second grade children scored well on major and dorian mode, the only other unfamiliar mode included in the study. Dittemore concluded that the nontonal criterion song was suited to the capabilities of sixth grade students of high musical aptitude.[41]

De Yarman reexamined the issue of difficulty of nontonal songs with very young children, of kindergarten and first grade, in a study to examine the effects of longer training in unique concepts emphasized in *ITML*. In the tonal portion of his study, De Yarman used control groups of students who were taught usual tonality: major and harmonic minor modes; and experimental groups who were also taught unusual tonality: nontonal patterns and songs in addition to major and harmonic minor modes. Criterion songs were adapted to include only basic patterns. De Yarman concluded that, overall, children of kindergarten and first grade could benefit from instruction in both tonal and nontonal music. Although there was little difference in performance on a nontonal criterion song, kindergarten children in the tonal-nontonal experimental group generally performed better than those in the control group on the major and minor songs. However, an interesting significant triple interaction occurred in performance of the minor criterion song. First grade students in the range of low aptitude in the tonal-nontonal experimental group scored considerably above those in the tonal-only control group, but the reverse was true for students of high tonal aptitude. First grade students of high aptitude whose training was only in major and minor scored above those whose training also included nontonal patterns and songs. Their scores were exceeded also by kindergarten children of high tonal aptitude in the experimental group. Curiously, in the first grade tonal-nontonal experimental group, students of low aptitude surpassed children of high tonal aptitude in performance on all three criterion songs, major, minor, and nontonal.[42] One might infer that, although nontonal training seemed to benefit kindergarten children, nontonal training was not beneficial to the slightly more advanced first grade students of high musical aptitude.

A following study by Miller also conducted with young children of first grade age, was designed to examine six variations in instructional objectives in tonal concepts. The study was basically of effects of amount and extent of training according to proportion of time allotted among tonal categories. Groups performed only in those criteria for which they had received specific training. The possibility of confounding tonal results with rhythmic difficulty was attenuated by adapting all criterion songs to utilize only basic patterns in triple meter. The only significant finding in the study was for a criterion song in minor, involving all groups. The control group, with only training in major and minor, performed significantly better than the group with major, minor, and nontonal training. Miller concluded that it is possible to devote too much time, in this case one-third of time allotted to tonal concepts, to nontonal patterns and songs resulting in actually hindering children's ability to sing in usual modes. The least effective training overall on modal criteria, observed on less familiar modal criteria, was for the group which had equally divided time among all seven concepts, major, minor, four less familiar modes, and nontonal patterns and songs. But for groups that had received additional training in only two less familiar modes, Miller found observably favorable results for major, minor, and the modes in which they were trained.[43] Results for all of the above studies tend to suggest that children can achieve in less familiar tonal concepts and that exposure may be of particular benefit to students of average and high aptitude. Relevant to this investigation is that both Dittemore's and Miller's results suggest that simple modal patterns, even though unfamiliar, may not be inherently difficult to perceive, but results from all three studies suggest that nontonal patterns may be inherently difficult to perceive.

As reactions to prior experience, results for the third and fourth comparisons of Level 5 in this study also reveal differences in aural perception of the two forms of unusual tonality. Scores for students in the third comparison group who had prior experience with test items in less familiar modes, were found to extend a modest improvement consistently throughout ranges of low and average achievement and students of highest achievement attained the ceiling of the test. Students of low achievement also found aural identification of test items in T_1, Level 5, easier after experience with Level 4, than did students of comparable rank in the first administration group, but scores for students of high achievement were considerably below those of the first administration group. Limitation to and extent of observed improvements among students of low and average achievement suggests that test items for Level 5, T_1, were perceived as easier than those of Level 3 or Level 4 because sounds of modal, and especially, nontonal patterns were unfamiliar.

ITML requirements in Levels 3 and 4, for subtest T_1, demand only differentiation of less familiar (modal or nontonal) sounds "unusual" from familiar sounds of major and minor "usual." In spite of the similar options for Levels 3 and 4, the task is quite different. Although generally unfamiliar and historically arbitrary, the aural impression of tonality can be objectively determined in less familiar modal patterns through harmonic implications, or diatonic characteristics — such as similar neighboring tone relationships between dominant and tonics within each less familiar mode. To discern whether patterns are unusual in Level 4, however, requires recognition of absence of tonality; by definition, nontonal has no objective tonality. That is, only subjectively can tonality be inferred for nontonal patterns due to their contrived, intervallic nature. Even if perceived as fleeting modulatory progressions, the effect is subjective. In this regard, it would seem that use of nontonal patterns could preclude any but short-term memory, analogous to nonsense syllables.

A tone pattern of successive dyads, arbitrarily arranged so as to obscure tonality, if recognized through pitch memory, contrived pattern progression, or by imputing intervallic modal relationships to separate intervals, would in any case involve extensive tonal associations. This would imply tonal sensitivity of a high order, and considerable achievement as well — a relationship between tonal aptitude and development of a sense of tonality as a meaningful reference for comparison and contrast.

The drop in scores for students of high achievement, following experience with nontonal test items in Level 4 suggest that a negative learning experience occurred, a more severe confusion for students of high tonal aptitude probably due to sensitivity to tonal organization and a lack of training in nontonal concepts. In the Dittemore study, a short term training period had resulted in the conclusion that sixth-grade students of high aptitude were capable of nontonal learning. This assumption could be inferred from norms offered for upper Levels of *ITML*, only for grades seven through twelve.

Considering similarity of correlations between parallel subtests of *Aural Perception* for Levels 1 and 2 and Levels 1 and 5, it is curious that students in the first comparison of Level 2 did not experience the same type of improvement. Neither was improvement shown in the first or second comparisons of Level 6, where tone patterns, like those in Levels 1 and 2, are comprised of major and minor, and further, are heard in keys of C and A. Tone patterns for Level 6 subtest items are heard with harmonic accompaniment of basic triads. As mentioned, Dittemore had found an interaction between high aptitude and higher grade level necessary to achievement in performance of a three-part song, whereas the task of subtest T_1 is one of aural recognition. Not only might one expect aural identification to be more certain because of harmonic accompaniment, but also, these same basic triads form the nucleus for simple tone patterns in Level 1.

Although this similarity is reflected in a high correlation for subtest T_1 between Levels 1 and 6 (see Table 9), no increment was found for scores in the first comparison. But, tone patterns superimposed on these basic triads heard in Level 6 subtest T_1 are complex as are those of Level 2. Because students had not been trained to acquire a vocabulary of tone patterns, it could have been pattern complexity which made identity of mode difficult to discern. The only effects "of consequence" observed for subtest T_1 were negative; found for the second comparison of Level 6, where complex patterns were heard in both Levels. Results confirm the identification of complexity of tone patterns assigned to *ITML* Levels 2 and 6.

Complexity of a tone pattern would seem to be in proportion to obscurity of tonal organization. That element which, by complexity, has been made imperceptible either dominant-to-tonic (harmonic) implication or resting tone, must be accounted for by aural imagery in order to impute musical meaning to a pattern. Further, to the extent that a person supplies harmony or resting tone, he is aurally imaging, even during the immediate perception of a tone pattern. Thus, recognition of distinguishing modal characteristics, although a function of achievement, conceivably would be dependent, in this respect, upon capacity for tonal imagery. This corroborates the function of aptitude to cope with complex elements of music; a relationship between capacity to aurally image and possible extent or pace of development in tonal achievement.

Particularly relevant to problems of curriculum are intercorrelation coefficients derived among subtests within a division. As mentioned, for each Level the musical materials, tonic patterns, are identical in test items of aural recognition and visual recognition, T_1 and T_2. It is of interest that, generally, less relationship is observed between the first two subtests in the *Tonal Concepts* division of the battery, than between the two subtests of literacy, T_2 and T_3, even though, because objectives for T_3 are less advanced, tone patterns for *Notational Understanding* are different from those found in *Reading Recognition*. Aural tasks and visual tasks are clearly separate dimensions of learning. *ITML* has been designed on the premise that achievement in aural identification of tone patterns should precede their visual identification. In reporting negative differences observed in the study, it was suggested that negative results found among higher Level subtests of literacy indicate lack of something basic to achievement. This writer infers from intercorrelations that advanced tonal literacy skills suffered for lack of association of aural meaning with visual symbols.

The writer also assumes from the relative size of correlation coefficients between second administration pairs of Levels that the most familiar task among subtests in the *Tonal Concepts* division of the battery was that of visual recognition of notation. Then, in order — writing notation, and least familiar of all — aural identification. In spite of apparent familiarity with the task of *Reading Recognition*, no improvement was found in any comparison of subtests of tonal literacy. High esteem for ability to read a musical score may bring about premature focus on visual skills, requiring emphasis on theoretical aspects of notation rather than recognition of musical meaning. Just as tonal symbols were developed for the apprentice musician as a reminder of what he already knew, a means of communication — their meaning must be supplied through imagery. The ability to image tonally has been established as a measure of tonal aptitude. It would seem profitable to investigate the order in which "levels" of tonal organization are perceived in relation to sequential objectives, as an indication of order in development of ability to supply through memory of the sound of patterns elements of relationship to tonality. It would also be profitable to compare relative ability to aurally image diatonic progressions and intervals and harmonic progressions.

Observations in this study are related to the use of tone patterns as musical "words." In a language, meaning can be interpreted in an objective or subjective sense. The analogy of "musical meaning" as used by this writer is applied to objective recognition of a tone pattern in relation to a sense of tonality — the underlying recognition of resting tone and implication of modal characteristics.

Results for subtests in the Tonal division of *ITML* raise questions of tonal aptitude and achievement crucial to teaching to the individual student. Is potential to achieve aurally, for example in tonal improvisation, different from potential to achieve in the use of tonal notation? Perhaps a different type of intelligence is involved in aural recognition of tone patterns and in understanding the theory of notational symbols. To the extent that musical potential is specific to aural imagery, aptitude would of necessity underlie literacy in a creative-interpretive sense, but perhaps only indirectly bear on visual skills.

Rhythmic Concepts

A more pronounced influence of prior experience was observed in the *Rhythmic Concepts* division of *ITML* in the effects of Levels 2 and 3 upon Levels 4 and 5. Criterion "learning effects" were found on subtest R_1, Rhythmic *Aural Perception*, Level 4 and Level 5 following both lower Levels 2 and 3. And, a positive influence was also observed in both Levels 4 and 5 on the two subtests of literacy skills, R_2, Rhythmic *Reading Recognition*, and R_3, Rhythmic *Notational Understanding*, but only after experience with Level 3. As can be seen in Tables 11 and 12, observed increments, substantial and widespread, are more extensive on Level 5 than on Level 4 and even more extensive following Level 3 than Level 2.

Positive differences of considerable magnitude were found in the second comparison of Level 4 for subtest R_1, *Aural Perception*. Increased scores, up to +9 standard score points, extended from the 25th through the 95th percentiles, average and high ranges of achievement. A parallel influence with even larger and more extensive improvement, up to +10 standard score points and from the 1st through the 95th percentiles, was found for subtest R_1 in the second comparison of Level 5. In both cases, the greatest discrepancy is to be seen at the 75th percentile. Similarly, large positive differences were found for subtest R_1 for third comparison groups of Levels 4 and 5. Increments are identical for average and high ranges of achievement in second and third comparisons of Level 4, and somewhat improved for students in the low range of achievement in the third comparison group. And similarly like the second, the third comparison group of Level 5 demonstrates consistent large improvement for subtest R_1, even for students in the lowest range of achievement.

The task required of students in subtest R_1 is to aurally identify the meter of rhythm patterns heard in subtest items by discriminating between two options. Aural identification of meter requires discernment of underlying organization of rhythm patterns. A pattern in rhythm is an arrangement of beats, a design of durations in time. By its nature, relationship among the sounds of a rhythm pattern requires a framework in segments of time, perceived as beats recurring in some order. According to Nettl:

> . . . The two predominant aspects of rhythm are dynamic and durational contrast. The fact that rhythm takes this two-dimensional form has probably been the root of the difficulty in defining and recognizing rhythm. Furthermore, it has four main facets, which are hierarchical and necessary for the identification of time relationships at various levels. The first is tempo: . . . The second facet is the study of the durational values of tones: . . . The third is meter, most simply defined as the recurrence of stressed points in contrast to unstressed ones. The fourth is the time relationship between larger sections.[44]

Gordon writes of the three-fold nature of rhythmic perception:

> As indicated, the three basic counterparts of rhythm — tempo beats, meter beats, and melodic rhythm — elicit musical meaning when the relationship between two or more notes (or rests) comprises a rhythmic pattern in the mind of the listener.[45]

What seems most pertinent to the process of learning to recognize and use musical rhythm is the statement that the *relationship . . . comprises a rhythmic pattern in the mind.* As in perception of tone, perception of sounds becomes musical — rhythmic perception — when at least three dimensions or levels are perceived or aurally imaged: an immediate or surface-level, the rhythm pattern as a unit; a deeper level, groupings of meter beats (commonly perceived in two's or three's in Western music); and the fundamental organizing level, the tempo beats (usually perceived as regularly recurring pairs of even beats, the "Tactus" of pre-symphonic times). Although the expression *levels* seems appropriate to awareness of rhythmic organization, in fact, one perceives divisions and subdivisions of varying lengths of time; meter is superimposed upon tempo by dividing the tempo beat; rhythm patterns divide or dispose and are superimposed upon meter beats. It would seem to be the function of aural imagery to perceive rhythmic organization by recognizing, or by supplying, these regularly recurring meter and tempo beats. Even though rhythm patterns may omit some sounds of regular organizing beats — so that they must be supplied through aural imagery — the beats recur to reestablish tempo and meter. For this reason, awareness of the three counterparts interacting in the organization of rhythm may be more readily perceptible aurally than their counterparts interacting in the organization of tonality.

Sequential objectives in the Levels of *ITML* are represented by recognition of specific meter categories together with degrees of complexity of rhythm patterns within these categories. Categories of meter designate interaction between tempo beats and meter beats; complexity occurs from interaction between rhythm patterns and meter. Because no terms are in common use to designate rhythmic perception by categories of meter[46] some options for subtest R_1, Rhythmic *Aural Perception*, are expressed in terms supplied by the test author.[47] Undoubtedly, subjects in this study encountered these unique terms for the first time in practice exercises preceding the subtests. More importantly for an examination of learning effects, students were not accustomed to aural identification of meter.

In Levels 1 and 2, test items are in fundamental categories of duple and triple meter. For subtest R_1 the student is expected to aurally recognize organization of even pairs of tempo beats and distinguish between their division in two's for duple meter and in three's for triple meter. This perception of fundamental tempo beats in even, regularly recurring pairs — common to both duple and triple meter, gives rise to the test author's term "usual" meter in Levels 3 and 4. In Level 3, R_1 options are "usual" and "mixed." The category mixed meter is a specific form of usual meter, but patterns are combinations of duple and triple meter; duplets inserted in triple meter and triplets in duple meter. In Level 4, options are "usual" and "unusual." Unusual meter may best be perceived as meter in which underlying tempo beats are altered to accommodate irregular groupings of meter beats — perhaps not paired, or not paired evenly, or quite irregular. For Levels 5 and 6, both options are categories unique to *ITML*, "mixed" and "unusual."

Of importance in considering influence of Levels 2 or 3 on the upper Levels 4 or 5, is the difficulty of rhythm patterns within categories. Instead of basic patterns heard in test items of Level 1, some subtest items in Level 2 are comprised of complex rhythm patterns including ties, syncopations, subdivisions and double dots. In Levels 3 and 4, some subtest items in usual meter are similarly complex. Rhythm patterns heard in mixed meter in Level 3 and in unusual meter in Level 4, although unfamiliar as categories, are simple in difficulty — heard as straightforward groupings of meter beats without additional divisions, subdivisions, or complexities. Level 5 test items in mixed or unusual meters are also comprised of rhythm patterns classified as "basic" in both categories. Mixed and unusual meters are not presented in complex patterns until Level 6.

As already discussed in relation to improved scores observed in T_1 in the comparisons of Level 5, results for R_1 in Levels 4 and 5 reflect subjects' lack of training in aural discrimination, and particularly, the lack of a vocabulary of rhythm patterns. Transfer of achievement acquired informally or through training not specifically to the objectives measured would, of course, direct this investigation to emphasize aspects of rhythmic aptitude rather than of rhythmic achievement.

As can be seen in the parallel design of Tonal and Rhythmic divisions of *ITML*, basic categories of duple and triple meter are grouped together as "usual meter" in the sense of familiar, in the manner of major and minor as "usual modes." The effect of grouping duple and triple together was undoubtedly a factor in resulting data, but it is assumed that differences observed in the effects of Level 3 and the effects on Level 4 were due to introduction of unfamiliar mixed and unusual meters. Questions regarding sequence of difficulty yet to be determined relate to phenomena of perception — whether categories of mixed and unusual meters are increasingly difficult to perceive, or just more-or-less familiar.

Results from the previously mentioned experimental studies by Dittemore and De Yarman are also relevant to rhythmic perception. In the Dittemore study of capabilities among elementary school children, scores over all grades were considerably lower for performance in mixed meter than in unusual meter, although interacting difficulty of tonal and rhythmic concepts in the criterion song may have been a factor. In relation to scores for students in higher grades, Dittemore found grade two suitable for study of mixed meter and grade three suitable for study of unusual meter.[48] De Yarman extended his study of effects of early exposure to year-long training in mixed and unusual meters. All preliminary instruction was in duple and triple meter, but kindergarten and first grade children who were also given training in songs and rhythmic activities in simple patterns of mixed and unusual meters were found to be more proficient in performance in all meters than students whose experience had been restricted to duple and triple meter.[49] This suggests that recognition of basic patterns in mixed or unusual meter may be a function of familiarity and training rather than remoteness inherent in perception of types or categories of meter.

The possibility of inherent difficulty in perception of unusual meter is somewhat like that of perception of unusual modes. What is natural to perception in the sense of mental organization, and what is influence of culture? For example, duple and triple meters seem basic. In fact scores for first grade students in the Dittemore study were higher on triple than duple meter.[50] Yet, triple meter patterns, stylized modes of mensural rhythm, were considered artistic sophistications in the thirteenth century. Unusual meter may represent arbitrary arrangements of rhythmic design of a sophisticated nature, reflecting achievement in manipulation of meter beyond basic duple and triple meter. Nonetheless, it is interesting that improvement in aural perception was found for two Levels in which the category unusual meter occurs.

The triplet, introduced in Level 3, which figures largely in recognition of mixed meter, was surely familiar to most eighth grade students in both first and second administration groups, whereas unusual meter groupings found in Levels 4 and 5 may have been quite unfamiliar to most subjects. Even so, aural identification of test items was found to be more demanding for Level 3 than for Levels 4 and 5. Differences between the two categories, usual and unusual meters, options for Levels 4 and 5, were no doubt more clearly identifiable than differences between two complex types of usual meter, as comprised in test items of Level 2, and particularly than between usual meter with complex rhythm patterns and the distinctly complex form of usual meter — mixed meter, found in test items in Level 3.

Aural identification of test items for Levels 4 and 5 could be made, for the usual meter option, by recognition of underlying pairs of tempo beats. Perhaps unusual meter could merely be identified as that which is not familiar; not organized in even pairs of tempo beats. After attention to the demands of test items in Level 2 or Level 3, students in second and third comparison groups of Levels 4 and 5, possessed of sufficient musical aptitude, may have learned to concentrate on underlying tempo and meter beats. Particularly, because rhythm patterns heard in mixed and unusual meters are not complicated with syncopations, subdivisions and ties until Level 6, they may have been able to improve aural recognition of test items in unusual meter, due to the basic, uncomplicated simplicity of rhythm patterns.

As shown in Table 12, an overview of subtest R_1 distributions in relation to options for successive Levels, listed in Figure 2, indicative of the scope of conceptual development within the battery, is pertinent to interpretation of results. Evidently simple patterns heard in Level 1 did not provide a learning situation in aural perception of duple and triple meter. Rather, after experience with Level 1, students of high achievement exhibited a negative effect on subtest R_1 in the upper Level 3. The difficulty of Level 3 is also apparent in the third comparison of Level 6, presumably due to extreme complexity of rhythm patterns in mixed and unusual meters comprised in subtest items of Level 6, but these negative effects were only demonstrated following Level 3. Although experience with Level 2 resulted in improved aural perception for second comparison groups of both Levels 4 and 5, as with Level 3, the severe negative effect on Level 6 which followed experience with Level 3 was not observed for the second comparison group. And, subjects in the second comparison group of Level 3 did not share the benefit of increased scores found in the second comparisons of Levels 4 and 5. Finally, perhaps most relevant to interpretation of improvement in standard score-percentile rank equivalents for second and third comparison groups on Levels 4 and 5, is that experience with Level 4 did not result in improved performance on Level 5.

Subjects in this study probably found unfamiliarity with unusual meter a less severe handicap than lack of proficiency in recognition of complex patterns. To distinguish between duple and triple meter in basic patterns requires attention to meter level in relation to fundamental tempo beats. To distinguish between complex forms of duple and triple meter, attention must be focused on intricacies of rhythm patterns as they relate to meter. To the extent that beats comprised in a rhythm pattern do not coincide with meter beats, the pattern becomes complex requiring aural imagery to maintain the meter. Mixed meter is a particular kind of complexity at the meter level, combining duple and triple meter within consistent tempo beats. That is, rhythm patterns in opposing meter, duplet or triplet, must be heard in relation to imperceptible consistent meter beats — a remembered meter — forming an aurally imaged miniature hemiola. When meter beats and/or tempo beats are obscured, the pattern becomes very complex. When meter beats and/or tempo beats are altered and obscured, the pattern becomes extremely complex. An example might be patterns with extended syncopations in mixed or unusual meter, found in Level 6.

Perhaps the memory for tempo is the essence of rhythmic imagery. If tempo is deliberately, entirely, obscured the result is arhythm. Arhythm, not a part of *ITML*, is akin to nontonal patterns, in which the resting tone is entirely obscured, so — devoid of tonality. Akin — but parallels are not exact: to be without tempo beats, an ongoing recognition, is to be without a standard of reference; to be without a resting tone is to be without a reference to tonality, but not without a standard of reference. In the test author's definition of "unusual tonal patterns," those which bear no *functional relationship* to any mode, it is not a single interval, or pair of tones, but the composite pattern which bears no functional relationship. Separately appended intervals might be associated with several modes, and identification is even possible as a collection of individual pitches. In effect, these alternatives for nontonal patterns are possible for nontonal patterns because of the standardization of pitch.

That is, although a single tone on any given pitch cannot indicate a mode, since Baroque times a standardized reference against which it can be compared has been available. Moreover, inherent within its own overtones are available the octave and dominant — historically the limits and defining outline of mode. In contrast, a single beat is not indicative of meter, but neither is there a standardized reference of speed against which even two beats, or the interval between them can be compared. In addition, two beats in succession are not necessarily representative of any specific level of rhythmic perception.

Further, modal characteristics are transferable to any pitch, and applicable within the pitch and its octave. This may not be so with meter. Meter characteristics, divisions of tempo beats, may be applicable only within ranges of speed. It remains to be determined whether an identical rhythm pattern, although theoretically applicable in mathematical ratio to any level of rhythmic perception, is actually aurally perceived at a level of rhythmic organization, meter or tempo, according to range of speed.

It would seem that size of tonal intervals in nontonal "unusual" patterns could therefore be related to objective associations even outside of tonality.

Conversely, that size of rhythmic intervals could not be remembered with precision except in relation to recognition of tempo beats.

Unusual meter, included in the three highest Levels of the *ITML* battery, and distinct from arhythm, is organized, but arbitrarily. An interesting possibility is that unusual meter may merely reflect larger groupings . . . that is, true tempo beats might exist, at least for some perceivers, regularly paired, but over a larger unit of time, as represented in the long-extinct proportional symbols, which permitted extension-in-depth to a fourth dimension, the "Maximodus." Perception of rhythm patterns of extended length may be a function of achievement, but limited by individual rhythmic aptitude.

In the function of aural imagery, related to "levels-in-depth" of rhythmic perception, it is possible that tempo beats in usual order — regularly recurring pairs of even duration — could represent a fundamental recognition. In that event, discrimination of basic patterns with altered tempo beats should be less difficult than discrimination of complexities at either the meter level or, especially at the surface-level of the rhythm pattern. This is because, while attending to surface complexity, aural imagery would be required to supply, when imperceptible, both meter and tempo beats. This implies that for untrained subjects test items in Level 3 in complex usual and basic mixed meters could be more difficult to aurally perceive than complex usual and unusual patterns in Level 4 and, especially, basic mixed and basic unusual meters in Level 5.

Results indicate that experience with test items in Level 2 or in Level 3 enhanced students' performance on Level 4 and to an even greater extent on Level 5, probably in proportion to their rhythmic aptitude. Also inferred from the data is that students in second and third comparison groups found the task of discrimination between categories of meter less exacting, and of coping with rhythm patterns comprised in test items less demanding in Levels 4 and 5 than in Level 2, or especially, Level 3. This is interpreted to be because discrimination of complex test items in Level 2 demanded use of aural imagery to supply meter beats and tempo beats while focusing on interaction between surface-level complexity and meter level. Likewise, similarity of underlying organization of tempo beats exacerbated the difficulty of discrimination in Level 3 test items, due to presentation of two types of complexity in usual meter, so that underlying tempo beats were regular for all test items. Also, both options in Level 3 encompassed duple and triple meter. In addition to requirements of aural imagery in complex items of duple and triple meter in the first option aural imagery was required in the second option, mixed meter, to discriminate the interplay of duple and triple meter.

Perhaps demands of attention to organization of meter and tempo experienced in Level 2 or in Level 3 contributed to increased scores on Levels 4 and 5. Following this experience, characteristics of different types of organization in usual and unusual meter may have become more obvious to students of high rhythmic aptitude. Because only basic patterns in unusual meter were used in Levels 4 and 5, attention could be focused on interaction between tempo beats and meter beats. The greater increase found for Level 5 than for Level 4 is probably due to use of only basic patterns in both mixed and unusual meters in Level 5.

In contrast to findings for subtest comparisons in the *Tonal Concepts* division of *ITML*, influence was also found on higher Level subtests of literacy in both Rhythmic *Reading Recognition* and Rhythmic *Notational Understanding*, R_2 and R_3. Sequential difficulties in visual skills include identification and use of rhythm patterns in the various categories of meter and of basic or complex difficulty presented visually in relation to increasing numbers of meter signatures and relative note-values.

A positive effect of +4 standard score points at the 50th percentile was observed in the first comparison of Level 5 on R_3, *Notational Understanding*, the only improvement found for a rhythmic subtest after experience with Level 1. Test content is not directly related between Levels 1 and 5. Rhythm patterns comprised in test items for Level 1 are simple patterns in duple or triple meter, written with either $\frac{2}{4}$ or $\frac{6}{8}$ meter signatures. In Level 5, test items are also simple, but are limited to unusual meter, using four different meter signatures, $\frac{3}{4}$, $\frac{5}{8}$, $\frac{7}{8}$, or $\frac{9}{8}$. Intercorrelation data is interpreted to suggest that students did not find commonality because of aural perception of rhythm patterns. What the students must have found in common, if not the feeling of rhythm patterns, was the appearance of notes. Due to the use of the eighth note to represent the meter beat in both Level 1 and Level 5, simple rhythm patterns are beamed together in obvious groupings of two's and three's. As reported in Table 9, correlation coefficients between Level 1 and 5 subtests, *Aural Perception*, R_1, $-.10$, and *Notational Understanding*, R_3, $+.40$, support the above interpretation

Following experience with Level 3, large improvements in scores were observed on the subtest of *Reading Recognition*, R_2, and on *Notational Understanding*, R_3, in the comparison of Level 4 and to a lesser extent, in the comparison of Level 5. Students in both third comparison groups had encountered in their first experience with subtest items for R_2 two sets of notational symbols: meter beats related to quarter notes and meter beats related to eighth notes. The same meter signatures utilized in subtest R_2, Level 3, are also found in test items in usual meter in R_2, Level 4. In addition, for subtest R_2, Level 4, six different meter signatures are introduced for items in unusual meter; but, students read rhythm patterns written with all of these unusual meter signatures in relation to eighth note meter beats. Also, because all test items in unusual meter for these Levels are simple in difficulty, they are written in groupings of two or three eighth notes beamed together (or as single flagged notes) so that meter groupings are readily visible. It is likely that subjects in this study were familiar with the use of quarter note meter beats with the tradition of common usage. The practice of beaming eighth notes in groupings of two's and three's apparently provides additional visual association for simple patterns. Evidently, students in third comparison groups were able to relate their improvement in aural perception of rhythm patterns to visual representation of simple rhythm patterns in unusual meter, comprised in test items of Level 4. The same increase in scores found for students of average and high achievement in the third comparison of Level 4 on subtest R_1 was also observed on subtest R_2.

Similarly high standard score-percentile rank equivalents were also found for the third comparison group of Level 4 on subtest R_3. Categories included in subtest items for Rhythmic *Notational Understanding*, R_3, are the same in Levels 3 and 4 — usual and mixed meter rhythm patterns. In Level 3, test items are written with eighth note meter beats and meter signatures $\frac{2}{4}$ and $\frac{6}{8}$. Added visual complexities for Level 4 subtest R_3 over requirements for Level 3 include test items written with either eighth note or quarter note meter beats, and the moderate difficulty of triplets with dotted rhythm patterns or duplets in divided meter beats. Score differences in the third comparison of Level 4 increased in magnitude according to achievement, to $+10$ standard score points from the 75th through the 99th percentiles.

Improvements were also found for subtests R_2 and R_3 in the third comparison of Level 5, although increments are not as great on R_2 nor as extensive on R_3 as those for Level 4. Higher scores for subtest R_2 were observed from the 1st through the 90th percentiles; the largest increase, $+7$ standard score points at the 40th percentile. For the third comparison of Level 5, R_3, higher scores are limited to $+4$ and $+5$ in the average and above average range. Students in both administration groups attained the highest possible score, 80, at the 99th percentile, thus preventing an increase for students of highest achievement.

Visual skills required in test items for Level 5, R_2, include identification of mixed and unusual meter rhythm patterns written with eleven different meter signatures; four for usual meter and seven for unusual meter. All rhythm patterns are basic; duplet and triplet groupings of usual meter are written either with quarter or with eighth notes, but all unusual meter patterns are written with eighth notes beamed together in groups of two's or three's. In contrast with Level 3, subtest items comprised in Level 5, R_3, are all unusual meter. As stated above, four different meter signatures are utilized in test items; the meter beat is in all cases an eighth note.

As noted in discussion of results from the Tonal division of the study, familiarity with the respective tasks of the three subtests in the Rhythmic division of the battery is demonstrated in Table 9. From higher correlations for the Rhythmic subtest, R_2, the writer infers that students are most familiar with the task of reading. Although difficulty was adjusted for subtests of writing skills, even writing seems more familiar to students than aural perception. The fundamental task of identifying "by ear" is shown to be least familiar for students overall.

As shown in Table 10, intercorrelation coefficients among Rhythmic subtests exhibit less relationship between R_1 and R_2, which measure aural perception and visual recognition of identical rhythm patterns, than between the two subtests of rhythmic literacy, R_2 and R_3, in which the musical content is not identical. Again, overall, it is the visual task which is common rather than aural imagery of rhythm patterns.

Possibly, lack of aural perception could be overlooked in the common practice of counting examples of rhythm. This traditional approach to visual presentation of rhythmic concepts logically relates to mathematical note-values. When confined to basic patterns, in which all components of rhythmic organization are represented — tempo beats, meter beats, and only simple variations within rhythm patterns, deficiencies may not be too evident. In addition to a problem already mentioned in regard to tonal notation (and in fact, to all written symbols) that symbols are a reminder of what one already knows, or highly related to something known well enough to transfer, there is another problem specific to rhythmic notation that hinders learning directly from visual symbols. Note values can be used at will to represent any level of rhythmic perception, tempo, meter, or divisions of meter beats in a rhythm pattern. Therefore, a note-value symbol does not inherently contain the musical meaning, relationship of the rhythm pattern to underlying organization of meter. The problem is like that of determining the meaning of a word in context. A profusion of meter signatures requires reading in sets of mathematical ratios. Chosen by a composer to indicate tempo, meter signatures are in no way standardized. To complicate higher achievement still further, the process of counting out a complex rhythm pattern is not only mathematically complicated, but demands that attention is focused on the surface level of rhythmic perception instead of on underlying organization of meter and tempo beats. Therefore, because availability of aural imagery is needed to supply meter and tempo in complex patterns, it seems possible that reliance on mathematical note-values could inhibit or hinder the demands of musical rhythm — particularly consistency of tempo. For example, no improvement was found among the five comparisons of Level 6 — both mixed and unusual meters are presented in complex rhythm patterns. Negative differences found for the second comparison of Level 6 substantiate the interpretation that complex rhythm patterns found in test items in both Level 2 and Level 6 preclude learning from visual symbols.

Rhythmic literacy — the meaningful use of visual symbols of rhythmic notation — requires ability to associate the feeling of a rhythm pattern, while recognizing its visual symbols in written notation. Ability to recognize the different organization of usual meter and unusual meter at the level of interaction between tempo beats and meter beats aurally, demonstrated in improved scores for students in the third comparison groups of Level 4 and Level 5, evidently provided aural skill necessary to improvement in subtests of Rhythmic literacy, R_2 and R_3. That is, evidence of general improvement in ability to aurally perceive rhythm by discriminating between the underlying rhythmic organization of usual and unusual meter, observed following Level 2 and Level 3, was followed, in consequence, by improvement on subtests R_2 and R_3 but following only Level 3.

Extremely high correlation coefficients between Levels 3 and 4 and Levels 3 and 5, found for subtests R_2 and R_3, could be a result of test content as perceived by the students. Although assuredly less familiar to students aurally, patterns of mixed meter and unusual meter limited to basic meter beats in Levels 4 and 5, are visually presented in familiar symbols: basic groupings of eighth notes.

Evidence of "learning effects" reported above seem to incorporate a common denominator: in aural recognition of rhythm patterns — basic groupings of meter beats in two's or three's; in visual recognition of rhythm patterns — representation of basic meter beat groupings written with eighth notes beamed together in two's or three's. Therefore, in view of the subjects' inexperience with aural recognition, demonstrated by over-all intercorrelation coefficients between R_1 and R_2, evidence of improved ability to aurally discriminate seems to be demonstrated in Level 4 and Level 5 after experience with Level 2 and Level 3. However, this improvement also seems specific to perception of the tempo beat level or organization of rhythm patterns presented in upper Level test items. In both lower Levels, discrimination is required between complex patterns of usual meter. In both upper Levels discrimination is required between usual and unusual meter. And, unusual meter is presented in Level 4 in basic patterns. Whereas usual meter patterns are complex in Level 2 for both categories, duple and triple; for the single category of usual meter in Levels 3 and 4, patterns are also complex; both categories, mixed and unusual, are simple patterns in Level 5.

This writer is inclined to the interpretation that observed improvement is at least largely related to rhythmic aptitude defined as ability to image interaction between tempo and meter. And, for students who possessed ability to aurally perceive rhythmic organization, that unusual meter was easier to identify in Level 4 and particularly in Level 5, due to the use of basic patterns, than usual meter previously experienced in Levels 2 and 3, but heard in complex patterns. This is supported by increased standard score-percentile ranks for students of low achievement in the comparisons of Level 5.

Evidence of transfer of aural improvement to recognition of visual symbols is displayed in the intercorrelation coefficient between R_1 and R_2 for the third comparison of Level 5 — the highest intercorrelation coefficient found for the fifteen comparisons of rhythmic subtests, .45. A lower intercorrelation coefficient, derived for the third comparison group on Level 4, .24, could reflect the use of some complex patterns in usual meter in that Level. Evidence from this study to indicate that visual skills can be improved, in a programmed learning sense, is limited to improvement as a consequence of improved aural identification. Further, it is limited to basic patterns in unusual meter and mixed meter and to use of visual symbols written with eighth notes beamed in groupings of two's and three's. That aural recognition of meter was improved at all ranges of achievement also corroborates emphasis on aural perception as prerequisite to transfer of tonal or rhythmic concepts to visual symbols which underlies the *ITML* battery.

One might question whether there is implied in improvement observed in Rhythmic *Aural Perception*, as opposed to less consequential improvement in Tonal *Aural Perception*, a relationship between rhythmic aptitude and ability to learn rhythmic organization which may not necessarily apply to tonal aptitude and tonal organization.

Summary of Interpretations

The writer interprets negative differences found for higher Levels of *ITML* to reflect: for Tonal and Rhythmic subtests of *Aural Perception* — lack of ability to cope with complex patterns aurally; and in subtests of literacy, Tonal and Rhythmic *Reading Recognition* and *Notational Understanding* — inability to associate "meaning" in the form of aural imagery with complex visual patterns.

Observations suggest that: (1) aural skills on the level of basic patterns may be amenable to improvement from listening to musical patterns, perhaps related to obviousness of resting tone or tempo beats; (2) visual skills require formal training. It remains to determine whether, and to what extent — given required achievement in aural recognition — visual skills might also be amenable to improvement in some programmed learning sense.

Questions related to development of sufficient achievement ability to aurally image fundamental tonal and rhythmic relationships as reference for comparison and contrast with advanced concepts, particularly unusual categories, might profitably be examined in studies with students who have been given opportunity to develop a vocabulary of complex patterns.

Most importantly, results indicate validity of the internal design of *ITML*, subtests in "sound before sight" order, and strongly indicate dependency of visual skills upon aural skills. The use of patterns as units of perception is logically validated in terms of sufficient information for recognition of the underlying organization of tonality or rhythm.

Finally:

(1) the relative difficulty of tone patterns or rhythm patterns among *categories* may be dependent upon familiarity;

(2) the relative difficulty of tone patterns or rhythm patterns by *complexity* may be dependent on the focus of aural perception on levels or organization of tonality or of rhythm;

(3) the usefulness of a vocabulary of tone patterns or rhythm patterns is dependent upon the extent to which the patterns can be aurally imaged.

Appendix

Table 13

Standard Score-Percentile Rank Equivalents for the
First Administration of *ITML* Level 2 and the
Second Administration of Level 2 Following Level 1

PR	Tonal Concepts					Rhythmic Concepts				Composite
	T_1	T_2	T_3	T	R_1	R_2	R_3	R	C
99	67* **68	70	70 71	68 69	69 68	70 69	80 80	72 71	67 67
95	63 64	67 66	66 67	64 65	64 64	65 64	80 80	68 67	64 64
90	60 61	64 62	63 64	61 62	60 60	61 60	80 80	65 64	61 61
85	57 58	61 59	61 62	59 59	57 57	58 56	80 80	63 61	59 58
75	55 56	58 57	59 60	56 57	54 55	55 53	80 79	61 59	57 56
60	52 53	56 55	57 58	54 55	51 52	52 50	79 78	59 57	56 55
50	49 51	54 53	55 56	52 53	49 49	50 48	77 76	57 55	55 54
40	47 48	52 51	52 53	50 51	46 46	48 45	74 73	56 54	54 53
25	44 45	49 49	49 50	48 49	43 42	45 42	68 69	54 53	52 51
15	41 42	47 46	46 46	46 46	39 38	42 39	63 64	52 51	50 49
10	37 38	44 43	42 42	44 43	35 34	38 35	58 59	49 49	48 47
5	33 34	40 40	37 38	41 40	30 29	33 31	53 54	46 46	46 45
1	30 30	36 37	32 33	37 37	25 24	28 26	48 48	42 42	43 43

*First Administration of Level 2
**Second Administration of Level 2 Following Level 1

Table 14

Standard Score-Percentile Rank Equivalents for the
First Administration of *ITML* Level 3 and the
Second Administration of Level 3 Following Level 1

PR	Tonal Concepts					Rhythmic Concepts				Composite
	T_1	T_2	T_3	T	R_1	R_2	R_3	R	C
99	70* **68	68	70	68	74 70	75 75	80 78	71 67	67 66
95	66 64	65	67 67	65 65	69 66	72 70	75 73	68 64	64 63
90	62 60	63	65 64	62 62	64 62	70 65	70 68	65 61	62 60
85	59 57	61	63 62	60 59	60 58	68 60	66 64	62 58	60 57
75	56 54	59	61 60	58 56	56 54	65 55	62 60	59 55	58 55
60	53 52	57	59 58	56 54	52 50	60 50	58 56	57 52	56 52
50	51 50	55	57 56	54 52	49 47	56 46	55 52	55 48	54 50
40	49 48	53	55 54	52 50	46 44	52 43	52 49	52 45	52 48
25	46 45	51	52 51	50 48	42 40	48 40	49 46	49 43	50 46
15	42 42	48	49 48	48 46	38 37	43 36	46 43	46 41	48 44
10	38 38	44	46 45	46 44	34 34	38 32	43 39	43 39	46 42
5	34 33	39	42 41	43 41	30 31	33 28	39 35	40 36	43 40
1	30 28	34	38 37	39 38	25 27	28 24	35 32	36 33	40 38
		29							

*First Administration of Level 3

Table 15

Standard Score-Percentile Rank Equivalents for the
First Administration of *ITML* Level 3 and the
Second Administration of Level 3 Following Level 2

PR	Tonal Concepts				Rhythmic Concepts				Composite
	T_1	T_2	T_3	T	R_1	R_2	R_3	R	C
99	70* **72	68 69	70 72	68 69	74 76	75 74	80 75	71 70	67 66
95	66 67	65 66	67 69	65 66	69 71	72 71	75 70	68 66	64 64
90	62 63	63 64	65 66	62 63	64 66	70 69	70 65	65 63	62 62
85	59 59	61 62	63 64	60 61	60 62	68 67	66 61	62 60	60 60
75	56 55	59 60	61 62	58 59	56 58	65 64	62 57	59 57	58 58
60	53 52	57 58	59 60	56 57	52 54	60 59	58 53	57 54	56 56
50	51 50	55 56	57 58	54 55	49 51	55 54	55 50	55 52	54 54
40	49 48	52 53	55 56	52 53	46 48	52 51	52 47	52 50	52 52
25	46 45	48 49	52 53	50 51	42 44	48 47	49 44	49 48	50 50
15	42 41	44 45	49 50	48 49	38 40	43 42	46 41	46 46	48 48
10	38 37	39 40	46 47	46 47	34 35	38 37	43 38	43 44	46 46
5	34 33	34 35	42 44	43 44	30 29	33 32	39 34	40 41	43 43
1	30 28	29 30	38 40	39 40	25 23	28 27	35 30	36 38	40 40

*First Administration of Level 3
**Second Administration of Level 3 Following Level 2

Table 16

Standard Score-Percentile Rank Equivalents for the First Administration of *ITML* Level 4 and the Second Administration of Level 4 Following Level 1

PR	Tonal Concepts								Rhythmic Concepts								Composite	
	T_1		T_2		T_3		T		R_1		R_2		R_3		R		C	
	71*	**73	65	67	80	80	67	68	71	73	64	63	65	67	63	64	61	62
99	71	73	65	67	80	80	67	68	71	73	64	63	65	67	63	64	61	62
95	66	67	61	62	75	75	64	62	65	67	58	57	61	63	58	59	58	58
90	61	62	57	57	71	70	61	57	59	61	53	52	57	59	54	55	55	54
85	57	57	53	52	67	66	58	53	54	56	49	48	54	56	51	52	53	51
75	53	53	50	48	64	62	55	49	50	52	46	45	52	53	49	50	51	49
60	50	50	47	44	61	58	52	46	47	49	44	43	50	51	47	48	49	47
50	47	47	45	42	58	55	50	44	45	47	43	42	48	49	45	46	48	46
40	45	45	42	39	55	52	49	43	43	45	41	40	46	47	43	44	47	45
25	42	42	39	36	51	48	47	41	41	42	38	37	44	45	41	42	45	43
15	39	39	36	33	46	43	45	39	38	38	35	34	41	42	39	39	43	41
10	36	35	34	30	40	37	43	36	34	33	32	31	37	38	36	35	41	39
5	32	30	31	27	33	30	40	33	29	27	29	28	33	33	33	32	39	37
1	28	25	27	23	25	22	36	29	23	21	25	24	28	27	30	28	37	35

*First Administration of Level 4
**Second Administration of Level 4 Following Level 1

Table 17

Standard Score-Percentile Rank Equivalents for the
First Administration of *ITML* Level 4 and the
Second Administration of Level 4 Following Level 2

PR	Tonal Concepts				Rhythmic Concepts				Composite
	T_1	T_2	T_3	T	R_1	R_2	R_3	R	C
99	71* / **69	65 / 64	80 / 80	67 / 66	71 / 73	64 / 63	65 / 68	63 / 66	61 / 62
95	66 / 64	61 / 60	75 / 75	64 / 63	65 / 69	58 / 57	61 / 64	58 / 61	58 / 58
90	61 / 59	57 / 56	71 / 70	61 / 60	59 / 65	53 / 52	57 / 60	54 / 57	55 / 55
85	57 / 55	53 / 52	67 / 66	58 / 57	54 / 62	49 / 48	54 / 56	51 / 54	53 / 53
75	53 / 51	50 / 49	64 / 63	55 / 54	50 / 59	46 / 45	52 / 53	49 / 52	51 / 51
60	50 / 48	47 / 46	61 / 60	52 / 51	47 / 56	44 / 43	50 / 50	47 / 50	49 / 49
50	47 / 45	45 / 44	58 / 57	50 / 49	45 / 53	43 / 42	48 / 48	45 / 48	48 / 48
40	45 / 43	42 / 41	55 / 54	49 / 48	43 / 50	41 / 41	46 / 46	43 / 46	47 / 47
25	42 / 40	39 / 38	51 / 50	47 / 46	41 / 46	38 / 39	44 / 44	41 / 44	45 / 45
15	39 / 37	36 / 35	46 / 45	45 / 44	38 / 41	35 / 36	41 / 41	39 / 42	43 / 43
10	36 / 34	34 / 33	40 / 39	43 / 42	34 / 35	32 / 33	37 / 37	36 / 39	41 / 41
5	32 / 30	31 / 30	33 / 32	40 / 39	29 / 27	29 / 30	33 / 33	33 / 36	39 / 39
1	28 / 26	27 / 26	25 / 24	36 / 35	23 / 20	25 / 27	28 / 28	30 / 33	37 / 37

*First Administration of Level 4
**Second Administration of Level 4 Following Level 2

Table 18

Standard Score-Percentile Rank Equivalents for the
First Administration of *ITML* Level 4 and the
Second Administration of Level 4 Following Level 3

PR	Tonal Concepts								Rhythmic Concepts								Composite	
	T_1*	T_1**	T_2		T_3		T		R_1		R_2		R_3		R		C	
99	71	71	65	65	80	80	67	68	71	73	64	72	65	75	63	68	61	62
95	66	66	61	61	75	74	64	64	65	69	58	66	61	71	58	65	59	59
90	61	62	57	58	71	69	61	60	59	65	53	61	57	67	54	62	55	57
85	57	58	53	55	67	64	58	56	54	62	49	57	54	64	51	59	53	55
75	53	54	50	52	64	60	55	53	50	59	46	54	52	61	49	57	51	54
60	50	51	47	49	61	56	52	50	47	56	44	52	50	58	47	55	49	53
50	47	48	45	47	58	52	50	48	45	53	43	51	48	55	45	53	48	52
40	45	46	41	43	55	48	49	47	43	50	41	49	46	52	43	51	47	50
25	42	43	39	41	51	44	47	45	41	46	38	46	44	48	41	48	45	47
15	39	40	36	38	46	39	45	43	38	42	35	42	41	44	39	44	43	44
10	36	37	34	36	40	34	43	41	34	37	32	37	37	39	36	39	41	41
5	32	33	31	33	33	28	40	38	29	31	29	31	33	33	33	34	39	38
1	28	29	27	29	25	22	36	34	23	25	25	25	28	26	30	28	37	35

*First Administration of Level 4
**Second Administration of Level 4 Following Level 3

Table 19

Standard Score-Percentile Rank Equivalents for the
First Administration of *ITML* Level 5 and the
Second Administration of Level 5 Following Level 1

PR	T₁ *	T₁ **	T₂	T₂	T₃	T₃	T	T	R₁	R₁	R₂	R₂	R₃	R₃	R	R	C	C
	Tonal Concepts								Rhythmic Concepts								Composite	
99	77	77	77	75	75	73	73	72	73	73	70	70	80	80	69	69	68	66
95	71	72	71	70	70	69	68	67	67	67	65	66	73	75	64	64	63	62
90	65	68	65	65	66	65	63	63	62	62	60	62	67	70	59	60	58	59
85	60	64	60	60	62	62	59	59	58	58	56	58	62	65	55	57	55	57
75	56	60	55	55	59	59	56	56	54	55	52	55	58	61	52	55	53	55
60	53	56	51	51	56	56	53	53	51	53	48	51	55	58	50	53	51	53
50	50	53	48	48	53	53	51	51	49	51	45	48	52	56	49	52	50	52
40	47	50	46	46	51	51	50	50	47	49	43	45	49	52	48	51	49	51
25	44	46	43	43	48	48	48	48	45	46	41	42	46	48	46	49	48	49
15	41	42	39	39	45	45	46	46	43	43	38	38	43	43	44	46	46	47
10	38	38	35	35	41	41	43	43	40	40	35	34	39	38	41	42	44	44
5	34	33	30	31	37	37	40	40	36	36	31	30	35	33	38	37	41	41
1	30	28	25	27	32	33	36	37	31	31	27	25	30	28	34	32	38	38

*First Administration of Level 5
**Second Administration of Level 5 Following Level 1

Table 20

Standard Score-Percentile Rank Equivalents for the
First Administration of *ITML* Level 5 and the
Second Administration of Level 5 Following Level 2

PR	Tonal Concepts					Rhythmic Concepts					Composite
	T_1	T_2	T_3	T	R_1	R_2	R_3	R	C
99	77* **75	77	75	73	73	71	73	70	70	80	80	69	69	68	68
95	71	71	71	70	68	67	67	71	65	65	73	73	64	65	63	65
90	65	67	65	65	63	63	62	69	60	60	67	67	59	61	58	62
85	60	63	60	60	59	59	58	67	56	56	62	62	55	58	55	58
75	56	60	55	55	56	56	54	64	52	52	58	58	52	55	53	58
60	53	57	51	53	53	54	51	61	48	48	55	55	50	53	51	55
50	50	54	47	51	51	52	49	58	45	45	52	53	49	52	50	53
40	47	51	44	48	48	50	47	55	43	43	49	50	48	51	49	52
25	44	47	41	45	45	48	45	52	41	41	46	46	46	49	48	51
15	41	43	38	42	42	46	43	49	38	38	43	42	44	47	46	50
10	38	39	35	39	39	43	40	45	35	35	39	38	41	44	44	48
5	34	35	30	37	36	40	36	41	31	31	35	34	38	41	41	43
1	30	30	25	32	32	36	31	36	27	27	30	29	34	37	38	40

*First Administration of Level 5
**Second Administration of Level 5 Following Level 2

Table 21

Standard Score-Percentile Rank Equivalents for the
First Administration of *ITML* Level 5 and the
Second Administration of Level 5 Following Level 3

PR	Tonal Concepts								Rhythmic Concepts								Composite	
	T_1		T_2		T_3		T		R_1		R_2		R_3		R		C	
	*	**	*	**	*	**	*	**	*	**	*	**	*	**	*	**	*	**
99	77	77	77	76	75	73	73	71	73	73	70	71	80	80	69	69	68	69
95	71	72	71	70	70	68	68	66	67	69	65	67	73	75	64	68	63	66
90	65	67	65	65	66	64	63	62	62	66	60	63	67	70	59	65	58	63
85	60	63	60	61	62	60	59	59	58	63	56	60	62	66	55	62	55	60
75	56	60	55	57	59	57	56	56	54	61	52	57	58	63	52	59	53	58
60	53	57	51	53	56	55	53	54	51	59	48	54	55	60	50	56	51	56
50	50	54	48	50	53	53	51	53	49	57	45	52	52	57	49	54	50	54
40	47	51	46	48	51	52	50	52	47	55	43	50	49	54	48	52	49	52
25	44	48	43	45	48	50	48	50	45	53	41	47	46	50	46	50	48	50
15	41	45	39	41	45	47	46	48	43	50	38	44	43	46	44	47	46	48
10	38	42	35	36	41	43	43	45	40	46	35	40	39	41	41	44	44	46
5	34	38	30	30	37	39	40	42	36	42	31	36	35	36	38	41	41	43
1	30	34	25	24	32	35	36	38	31	37	27	31	30	30	34	37	38	39

*First Administration of Level 5
**Second Administration of Level 5 Following Level 3

Table 22

Standard Score-Percentile Rank Equivalents for the First Administration of *ITML* Level 5 and the Second Administration of Level 5 Following Level 4

	Tonal Concepts					Rhythmic Concepts				Composite
PR	T_1	T_1	T_2	T_2	T_3	T_3	T	R_1	R_1	R_2	R_2	R_3	R_3	R	R	C	C
99	77*	**77	77	69	75	67	73	68	73	73	70	68	80	74	69	66	68	65
95	71	68	71	64	70	63	68	64	67	68	65	62	73	69	64	62	63	61
90	65	65	65	59	66	59	63	60	62	63	60	57	67	64	59	58	58	58
85	60	62	60	55	62	55	59	56	58	59	56	52	62	60	55	55	55	55
75	56	59	55	51	59	52	56	53	54	55	52	48	58	57	52	53	53	53
60	53	57	51	48	56	49	53	51	51	52	48	45	55	54	50	51	51	51
50	50	55	48	45	53	47	51	50	49	50	45	43	52	52	49	49	50	49
40	47	53	46	43	51	45	50	49	47	49	43	42	49	50	48	48	49	48
25	44	50	43	41	48	42	48	47	45	47	41	41	46	47	46	47	48	46
15	41	46	39	38	45	39	46	43	43	45	38	39	43	43	44	45	46	44
10	38	41	35	35	41	35	43	41	40	42	35	37	39	38	41	43	44	42
5	34	36	30	31	37	30	40	38	36	38	31	34	35	33	38	40	41	40
1	30	30	25	27	32	25	36	34	31	34	27	30	30	27	34	37	38	38

*First Administration of Level 5
**Second Administration of Level 5 Following Level 4

Table 23

Standard Score-Percentile Rank Equivalents for the
First Administration of *ITML* Level 6 and the
Second Administration of Level 6 Following Level 1

PR	Tonal Concepts						Rhythmic Concepts						Composite	
	T_1	T_1**	T_2	T_3		T	R_1	R_1	R_2	R_2	R_3	R		C
99	70*	**70	76	74	74	71	69	66	70	70	68	65	80	78	68	65	68	65
95	66	65	70	68	69	66	65	62	66	66	64	61	74	74	64	62	65	62
90	62	61	65	63	64	61	62	59	62	62	61	58	68	68	61	59	62	59
85	59	57	61	59	60	57	59	56	58	58	58	55	63	64	58	56	59	56
75	56	54	58	56	57	54	56	53	55	54	55	52	59	61	56	53	56	53
60	54	52	55	53	54	51	53	50	53	51	52	49	56	58	54	51	53	50
50	52	50	52	50	52	49	51	48	51	48	50	47	53	55	52	49	51	48
40	49	47	49	47	50	47	50	47	48	45	48	45	51	53	50	47	50	47
25	46	44	46	44	47	44	48	45	45	42	46	43	48	50	48	45	48	46
15	42	40	42	41	43	41	46	43	42	39	43	41	44	46	46	43	46	45
10	38	36	37	37	39	37	43	41	38	36	39	38	40	42	42	40	44	43
5	33	31	32	33	34	33	39	39	33	33	34	34	35	37	38	38	41	41
1	27	25	26	29	29	29	35	37	27	29	28	30	29	31	33	35	37	39

*First Administration of Level 6
**Second Administration of Level 6 Following Level 1

Table 24

Standard Score-Percentile Rank Equivalents for the
First Administration of *ITML* Level 6 and the
Second Administration of Level 6 Following Level 2

PR	Tonal Concepts					Rhythmic Concepts					Composite
	T_1	T_2	T_3	T	R_1	R_2	R_3	R	C
	70* **70	76 75	74 72	69 67	70 70	68 68	80 78	68 67	68 66
99	66 65	70 69	69 67	65 63	66 66	64 64	74 73	64 63	65 63
95	62 60	65 64	64 62	62 59	62 62	61 60	68 69	61 60	62 60
90	59 56	61 59	60 58	59 56	58 59	58 56	63 65	58 57	59 57
85	56 52	58 55	57 54	56 53	55 56	55 53	59 62	56 55	56 54
75	54 49	55 51	54 51	53 50	53 54	52 50	56 59	54 53	53 51
60	52 46	52 48	52 49	51 48	51 52	50 47	53 56	52 51	51 49
50	49 43	49 46	50 47	50 47	48 49	48 45	51 53	50 49	50 48
40	46 40	46 43	47 44	48 45	45 46	46 43	48 49	48 46	48 46
25	42 37	42 40	43 40	46 43	42 42	43 40	44 44	46 43	46 44
15	38 33	37 36	39 36	43 40	38 38	39 36	40 38	42 39	44 42
10	33 29	32 31	34 32	39 36	33 33	34 31	35 32	38 35	41 39
5	27 25	26 26	29 28	35 32	27 27	28 25	29 26	33 30	37 35
1									

*First Administration of Level 6
**Second Administration of Level 6 Following Level 2

Table 25

Standard Score-Percentile Rank Equivalents for the
First Administration of *ITML* Level 6 and the
Second Administration of Level 6 Following Level 3

PR	Tonal Concepts						Rhythmic Concepts				Composite	
	T_1	T_2	T_3			T	R_1	R_2	R_3	R	C	
99	70*	76	75	74	71	69	68	70	68	68	80	78	68	68	66
95	66	**69	70	69	66	65	64	66	64	64	74	73	64	63	65	63
90	62	65	65	64	61	62	60	62	61	61	68	69	61	60	62	60
85	59	62	61	60	57	59	57	58	58	58	63	65	58	57	59	57
75	56	59	58	57	54	56	54	55	55	56	59	62	56	54	56	54
60	54	56	55	54	51	53	51	53	52	54	56	59	54	52	53	51
50	52	53	52	52	49	51	49	51	50	52	53	56	52	49	51	49
40	49	50	50	50	47	50	48	48	48	50	51	53	50	46	50	48
25	46	47	47	47	43	48	46	45	46	48	48	50	48	44	48	46
15	42	44	44	43	39	46	44	42	43	46	44	46	46	41	46	44
10	38	40	40	39	35	43	41	38	39	42	40	41	42	38	44	42
5	33	36	35	34	30	39	38	33	34	38	35	36	38	35	41	40
1	27	31	30	29	25	35	34	27	28	33	29	30	33	33	37	38

*First Administration of Level 6
**Second Administration of Level 6 Following Level 3

Table 26

Standard Score-Percentile Rank Equivalents for the
First Administration of *ITML* Level 6 and the
Second Administration of Level 6 Following Level 4

PR	Tonal Concepts				Rhythmic Concepts				Composite
	T_1	T_2	T_3	T	R_1	R_2	R_3	R	C
99	70* **68	76 74	74 68	69 66	70 67	68 65	80 78	68 65	68 65
95	66 64	70 68	69 64	65 62	66 63	64 61	74 73	64 61	65 62
90	62 61	65 63	64 60	62 59	62 60	61 58	68 68	61 58	62 59
85	59 58	61 59	60 57	59 56	58 57	58 55	63 64	58 56	59 56
75	56 55	58 55	57 54	56 53	55 54	55 52	59 61	56 54	56 54
60	54 52	55 53	54 51	53 50	53 52	52 49	56 58	54 52	53 52
50	52 49	52 50	52 48	51 48	51 50	50 47	53 56	52 51	51 50
40	49 46	49 47	50 46	50 46	48 48	48 45	51 53	50 50	50 48
25	46 43	46 44	47 44	48 44	45 45	46 43	48 49	48 49	48 46
15	42 40	42 40	43 41	46 42	42 42	43 40	44 45	46 47	46 44
10	38 36	37 35	39 38	43 40	38 38	39 37	40 40	42 43	44 42
5	33 31	32 30	34 35	39 38	33 33	34 34	35 35	38 39	41 40
1	27 25	26 24	29 32	35 36	27 28	28 30	29 30	33 34	37 38

*First Administration of Level 6
**Second Administration of Level 6 Following Level 4

Table 27

Standard Score-Percentile Rank Equivalents for the
First Administration of *ITML* Level 6 and the
Second Administration of Level 6 Following Level 5

	Tonal Concepts				Rhythmic Concepts				Composite	
PR	T_1	T_2	T_3	T	R_1	R_2	R_3	R	C	
99	70* **70	76 76	74 75	69 70	70 70	68 69	80 79	68 69	68	69
95	66 65	70 69	69 68	65 66	66 66	64 65	74 74	64 65	65	65
90	62 61	65 64	64 62	62 62	62 62	61 60	68 69	61 61	62	61
85	59 57	61 60	60 57	59 58	58 58	58 56	63 64	58 58	59	57
75	56 54	58 57	57 54	56 55	55 55	55 52	59 60	56 55	56	54
60	54 51	55 54	54 52	53 52	53 53	52 49	56 57	54 53	53	52
50	52 49	52 51	52 50	51 50	51 51	50 46	53 55	52 51	51	50
40	49 47	49 48	50 48	50 48	48 48	48 44	51 52	50 49	50	49
25	46 45	46 45	47 45	48 46	45 45	46 41	48 48	48 47	48	47
15	42 42	42 41	43 42	46 44	42 42	43 38	44 43	46 45	46	45
10	38 38	37 36	39 38	43 42	38 38	39 35	40 38	42 41	44	43
5	33 34	32 31	34 34	39 39	33 33	34 32	35 33	38 37	41	40
1	27 29	26 25	29 30	35 35	27 28	28 28	29 28	33 32	37	36

*First Administration of Level 6
**Second Administration of Level 6 Following Level 5

Notes

Thelma Volger is a research fellow and adjunct lecturer in the Department of Psychology, State University of New York at Buffalo. Beginning in February 1976 she will be a senior lecturer in music education at Churchlands Teachers College, Western Australia.

1 William E. Whybrew, *Measurement and Evaluation in Music*, 2nd ed. (Dubuque, Iowa: Wm. C. Brown, 1971), p. 2.
2 Paul R. Lehman, *Tests and Measurements in Music* (Englewood Cliffs, N.J.: Prentice-Hall, 1971).
3 Whybrew, p. 149.
4 Lehman, p. 57.
5 Edwin Gordon, *The Psychology of Music Teaching* (Englewood Cliffs, N.J.: Prenctice-Hall, 1971), p. 62.
6 Claude Palisca, ed., "Music in Our Schools, a Search for Improvement," *Yale Seminar Report* (Washington, D.C.: Office of Education, Comprehensive Research Program, 1963), p. 12.
7 Palisca, p. 12.
8 Palisca, p. 29.
9 Robert Mager, *Preparing Instructional Objectives* (Palo Alto, Calif.: Fearon, 1962).
10 Jerome S. Bruner, *The Process of Education* (New York: Random House, Vintage ed., 1963), pp. 5–7.
11 Grosvenor Cooper, and Leonard B. Meyer, *The Rhythmic Structure of Music* (Chicago: University of Chicago Press, Phoenix ed., 1963), p. 1.
12 Gordon, *The Psychology of Music Teaching*, p. 66.
13 Edwin Gordon, *Iowa Tests of Music Literacy* (Iowa City: University of Iowa, 1971).
14 Hereafter, *Iowa Tests of Music Literacy* is cited as *ITML*.
15 Gordon, *The Psychology of Music Teaching*, pp. 66, 67.
16 Edwin Gordon, *Musical Aptitude Profile* (Boston, Mass.: Houghton-Mifflin, 1965).
17 Hereafter, *Musical Aptitude Profile* is cited as *MAP*.
18 Gordon, *The Psychology of Music Teaching*, p. 130.
19 Edwin Gordon, *Manual, Iowa Tests of Music Literacy* (Iowa City: Bureau of Educational Research and Service, University of Iowa, 1971), p. 1.
20 Subtests T_1, T_2, R_1, and R_2 also include an "In-Doubt Option." See footnote 37.
21 Gordon, *Manual, ITML*, pp. 1–2.
22 Warren C. Swindell, "An Investigation of the Adequacy of the Content and Difficulty Levels of the *Iowa Tests of Music Literacy*" (Ph.D. diss., University of Iowa, 1970).
23 James L. Mohatt, "A Study of the Validity of the *Iowa Tests of Music Literacy*," *Experimental Research in the Psychology of Music: 7*, Studies in the Psychology of Music, Vol. 7 (Iowa City: University of Iowa Press, 1971), pp. 144–167.
24 Robert W. Thayer, "An Investigation of the Interrelation of Personality Traits, Musical Achievement and Different Measures of Musical Aptitude," *Experimental Research in the Psychology of Music: 8*, Studies in the Psychology of Music, Vol. 8 (Iowa City: University of Iowa Press, 1972), pp. 103–118.
25 Stanley Schleuter, "An Investigation of the Interrelation of Personality Traits, Musical Aptitude and Musical Achievement," *Experimental Research in the Psychology of Music: 8*, Studies in the Psychology of Music, Vol. 8 (Iowa City: University of Iowa Press, 1972), pp. 90–102.
26 Roger V. Foss, "An Investigation of the Effect of the Provision of the 'In Doubt' Response in the Validity of the *Iowa Tests of Music Literacy*," (Ph.D. diss., University of Iowa, 1972).
27 Edgar E. Dittemore, "An Investigation of Some Musical Capabilities of Elementary School Students," *Experimental Research in the Psychology of Music*, Studies in the Psychology of Music, Vol. 6 (Iowa City: University of Iowa Press, 1970), pp. 1–44.
28 Robert M. De Yarman, "An Experimental Analysis of the Development of Rhythmic and Tonal Capabilities of Kindergarten and First Grade Children," *Experimental Research in the Psychology of Music: 8*, Studies in the Psychology of Music, Vol. 8 (Iowa City: University of Iowa Press, 1972), pp. 1–44.
29 Philip H. Miller, "An Experimental Analysis of the Development of Tonal Capabilities of First Grade Children," *Experimental Research in the Psychology of Music: 10*, Studies in the Psychology of Music, Vol. 10 (Iowa City: University of Iowa Press, 1973).

30 Gordon, *Manual, ITML*, p. 2.
31 Mohatt, *Validity Study, ITML*, p. 41.
32 Mohatt, *Validity Study, ITML*, p. 34.
33 Experimental groups for a five-year study undertaken by the test author were also selected from the Des Moines school system. Those students, all band members, did not attend general music classes. Reports for second and third years appear in the series *Studies in the Psychology of Music*, Vols. 8 and 9 (Iowa City: University of Iowa Press, 1972, 1973), Edwin Gordon ". . . Results of a Five-Year Longitudinal Study of the Musical Achievement of Culturally Disadvantaged Students."
34 Based on information from Elementary and Secondary School Act of 1965, Title I.
35 Gordon, *Manual, ITML*, Standard scores for *ITML* range from 20 through 80.
36 Gordon, *Manual, ITML*, Table 8, pp. 100–105.
37 In addition to the two response options of mode or meter in T_1 and R_1 and the two response options, Yes, or No, in T_2 and R_2, an additional response option "In-Doubt" is offered in the *ITML* battery.
38 Foss, *Validity Study*, p. 60.
39 Gordon, *The Psychology of Teaching Music*, p. 91.
40 Gordon, *Psychology*, p. 113. "Comprehensive music appreciation includes, and is contingent on music appreciation readiness — on an aural and kinesthetic *understanding* of the tonal and rhythmic aspects of music."
41 Dittemore, "An Investigation of Some Musical Capabilities . . . ," p. 31.
42 De Yarman, "An Experimental Analysis of the Development of Tonal Capabilities . . . ," pp. 31–32.
43 Miller, "An Experimental Analysis of the Development of Tonal Capabilities . . . ."
44 Bruno Nettl, *Music in Primitive Culture* (Cambridge, Mass.: Harvard University Press, 1956), pp. 61, 62.
45 Gordon, *Psychology*, p. 69. For the term "melodic rhythm," see p. 21. In this study the term rhythm pattern is substituted for melodic rhythm or rhythmic pattern.
46 Curt Sachs, *Rhythm and Tempo* (New York: W. W. Norton, 1953). Terms used by Sachs have not received acceptance, even in subsequent publications concerning musical theory. He did, however, use the terms "divisive" for duple divisions, and "additive" which seems to indicate not only triple but also larger subdivisions, perhaps to allow for groupings such as Gordon includes in the category, "Unusual."
47 See Figure 2.
48 Dittemore, "An Investigation of Some Musical Capabilities . . . ," p. 18.
49 De Yarman, "An Experimental Analysis of the Development of Tonal Capabilities . . . ," p. 32.
50 Dittemore, "An Investigation of Some Musical Capabilities . . . ," p. 19.

BIBLIOGRAPHY

Bruner, Jerome S. *The Process of Education*. New York: Random House, Vintage Books, 1963.

———. *Toward a Theory of Instruction*. Cambridge, Mass.: Harvard University Press, 1966.

Bugelski, Bergen R. *The Psychology of Learning Applied to Teaching*. Indianapolis: Bobbs-Merrill, 1973.

Buros, Oscar K., ed. *Seventh Mental Measurements Yearbook*. Highland Park, N.J.: Gryphon Press, 1972.

Colwell, Richard. "The Development of the Music Achievement Test Series." *Council for Research in Music Education*, Bulletin No. 22 (Fall 1970):57–72.

──────.*The Evaluation of Music Teaching and Learning*. Englewood Cliffs, N.J.: Prentice-Hall, 1970.

──────. *MAT Music Achievement Tests, Interpretive Manual*. Chicago: Follett Educational Corporation, 1969.

Cooper, Grosvenor, and Meyer, Leonard B. *The Rhythmic Structure of Music*. Chicago: University of Chicago Press, Phoenix Books, 1963, 1960.

Cronbach, Lee J. *Essentials of Psychological Testing*, 2nd ed. New York: Harper, 1960.

De Yarman, Robert M. "An Experimental Analysis of the Development of Rhythmic and Tonal Capabilities of Kindergarten and First Grade Children." *Experimental Research in the Psychology of Music: 8*. Studies in the Psychology of Music, vol. 8. Iowa City: University of Iowa Press, 1972.

Dittemore, Edgar E. "An Investigation of Some Musical Capabilities of Elementary School Students." *Experimental Research in the Psychology of Music*. Studies in the Psychology of Music, vol. 6. Iowa City: University of Iowa Press, 1970.

Foss, Roger V. "An Investigation of the Effect of the Provision of the 'In Doubt' Response on the Validity of the *Iowa Tests of Music Literacy*." Ph.D. dissertation, University of Iowa, 1972.

Ginsburg, Herbert, and Opper, Sylvia. *Piaget's Theory of Intellectual Development, An Introduction*. Englewood Cliffs, N.J.: Prentice-Hall, 1969.

Gordon, Edwin, ed. "A Selected Bibliography of Experimental Research Studies in the Psychology of Music from 1937 through 1970." *Experimental Research in the Psychology of Music: 7*. Studies in the Psychology of Music, vol. 7. Iowa City: University of Iowa Press, 1971.

──────. "A Selected Bibliography of Experimental Research Studies in the Psychology of Music for 1971." *Experimental Research in the Psychology of Music: 8*. Studies in the Psychology of Music, vol. 8. Iowa City: University of Iowa Press, 1972.

──────. *How Children Learn When They Learn Music*. Iowa City: Edwin Gordon, 1968.

──────. *Iowa Tests of Music Literacy*. Iowa City: University of Iowa, 1971.

──────. *Musical Aptitude Profile*. Boston: Houghton Mifflin, 1965.

──────. *The Psychology of Music Teaching*. Englewood Cliffs, N.J.: Prentice-Hall, 1971.

Lehman, Paul R. *Tests and Measurements in Music*. Englewood Cliffs, N.J.: Prentice-Hall, 1968.

Leonhard, Charles. "Evaluation in Music Education." In *Basic Concepts in Music Education*, the Fifty-seventh Yearbook of the National Society for the Study of Education, Part I, ed. Nelson B. Henry. Chicago: National Society for the Study of Education, 1958.

Lindquist, E. F. *Design and Analysis of Experiments*. Boston: Houghton Mifflin, 1953.

Mager, Robert F. *Preparing Instructional Objectives*. Palo Alto, Calif.: Fearon, 1962.

Mohatt, James L. "A Study of the Validity of the *Iowa Tests of Music Literacy*." *Experimental Research in the Psychology of Music: 7*. Studies in the Psychology of Music, vol. 7. Iowa City: University of Iowa Press, 1971.

Music Educators National Conference. *The Study of Music in the Elementary School: A Conceptual Approach*. Washington, D.C.: Music Educators National Conference, 1967.

Nettl, Bruno. *Music in Primitive Culture*. Cambridge, Mass.: Harvard University Press, 1956.

Palisca, Claude, ed. "Music in Our Schools, A Search for Improvement." Yale Seminar

Report. Washington, D.C.: Office of Education, Comprehensive Research Program, 1963.
Piaget, Jean. *Science of Education and the Psychology of the Child.* Trans. by Derek Coltman. New York: Viking Press, 1971.
Reimer, Bennett. "Effects of Music Education." *Perspectives in Music Education,* Source Book III. Washington, D.C.: Music Educators National Conference, 1966.
Sachs, Curt. *Rhythm and Tempo.* New York: W. W. Norton, 1953.
Schleuter, Stanley. "A Study of the Interrelationship of Personality Traits, Musical Aptitude, and Musical Achievement." *Experimental Research in the Psychology of Music: 8.* Studies in the Psychology of Music, vol. 8. Iowa City: University of Iowa Press, 1972.
Schneider-Cady. *Evaluation and Synthesis of Research Studies Relating to Music Education.* ERIC ED 010 298, 1965.
Seashore, Carl E. *Psychology of Music.* New York: McGraw-Hill, 1938.
Swindell, Warren C. "An Investigation of the Adequacy of the Content and Difficulty Levels of the *Iowa Tests of Music Literacy.*" Ph.D. dissertation, University of Iowa, 1970.
Tate, Merle. *Statistics in Education and Psychology.* New York: Macmillan, 1971.
Thayer, Robert. "An Investigation of the Interrelation of Personality Traits, Musical Achievement, and Different Measures of Musical Aptitude." *Experimental Research in the Psychology of Music: 8.* Studies in the Psychology of Music, vol. 8. Iowa City: University of Iowa Press, 1972.
Thomas, Ronald. *A Study of New Concepts, Procedures, and Achievements in Music Learning as Developed in Selected Music Education Programs.* Washington, D.C.: Department of Health, Education and Welfare. Office of Education, Bureau of Research, ED 003–126, 1966.
Thorndike, Robert and Hagen, Elizabeth. *Measurement and Evaluation in Psychology and Education.* New York: John Wiley, 1969.
Whybrew, William E. *Measurement and Evaluation in Music.* Dubuque, Iowa: William C. Brown, 1971.

A SELECTED BIBLIOGRAPHY OF EXPERIMENTAL RESEARCH STUDIES IN THE PSYCHOLOGY OF MUSIC

The following entries for 1968 through 1972 are intended to update the bibliographies in Volumes 7 through 9 of the Series. The first extended bibliography is found in Volume 7, covering the years 1937 through 1970. In addition to this updating, the selected bibliography for 1973 is given at the end.

1968

McLeish, John. *The Factor of Musical Cognition in Wing's and Seashore's Tests.* London: Novello and Company, 1968.

Noy, Pinchas. "The Development of Musical Ability." *Psychoanalytic Study of the Child* 23 (1968):332–347.

1969

Bruton-Simmonds, I. V. "A Critical Note on the Value of the Seashore Measures of Musical Talents." *Psychologia Africana* 13 (1969):50–54.

Nichols, Alan C. "Correlations Between Timbre Discrimination and Articulation Scoring." *Speech Monographs* 36 (1969):148–151.

Polakowski, Krzysztof. "The Concepts of Musicality." *Psychologia Wychowawcza* 12 (1969):421–433.

Uherik, Anton, and Kuric, Jozef. "Perception of Musical Stimuli and the Bioelectric Response of the Skin." *Psychologia A Patopsychologia Dietata* 4 (1969):299–306.

1970

Gordon, H. W. "Hemispheric Asymetries in the Perception of Musical Chords." *Cortex* 6 (1970):387–398.

Hickman, Aubrey. "Experiments With Children Involving Pitch, Rhythm, and Timbre." *Research in Education* 3 (1970):73–86.

McDonald, Marjorie. "Transitional Tunes and Musical Development." *Psychoanalytic Study of the Child* 25 (1970):503–520.

Parker, D. H. "Musical Perception and Backwardness in Reading." *Educational Research* 12 (1970):244–246.

Stafford, R. E. "Estimation of the Interaction Between Heredity and Environment for Musical Aptitude of Twins." *Human Heredity* 20 (1970):356–360.

1971

Bradshaw, John L., Nettleton, Norman C., and Gina Geffen. "Ear Differences and Delayed Auditory Feedback: Effects on a Speech and a Music Task." *Journal of Experimental Psychology* 91 (1971):85–92.

Chimielewska, Elzibieta. "Effectiveness of Single-Handed and Dual-Handed Learning of Piano Works." *Psychologia Wychowawcza* 14 (1971):465–474.

Cuddy, Lola L. "Absolute Judgment of Musically-Related Pure Tones." *Canadian Journal of Psychology* 25 (1971):42–55.

Davies, J. B. "New Tests of Musical Aptitude." *British Journal of Psychology* 62 (1971):557–565.

Doehring, Donald G., and Ling, Daniel. "Matching to Sample of Three-Tone Simultaneous and Successive Sounds by Musical and Nonmusical Subjects." *Psychonomic Science* 25 (1971):103–105.

Dowling, W. J. "Recognition of Inversions of Melodies and Melodic Contours." *Perception and Psychophysics* 9 (1971):348–349.

Dowling, W. J., and Fujitani, Diane S. "Contour, Interval, and Pitch Recognition in Memory for Melodies." *Journal of the Acoustical Society of America* 49 (1971):524–531.

Greenberg, Roger P., and Fisher, Seymour. "Some Differential Effects of Music on Projective and Structured Psychological Tests." *Psychological Reports* 28 (1971):817–818.

Il'ina, G. A., and Rudneva, S. D. "The Mechanics of Musical Experience." *Voprosy Psikhologii* 17 (1971):66–74.

Mochizuki, Minoru. "A Study About the Relationship Between the Variability of the Menta Tempo and the Musical Talent Test." *Journal of Child Development* 7 (1971):48–53.

Vibert, Paule, and Breskin-Aleinick, Nadine. "A Genetic Study of the Organization of Hearing Through the Perception of Musical Patterns With Elementary Structures: Inversion, Transposition, Transposed Inversion." *Psychologica Belgica* 11 (1971):133–143.

Wilcox, Roger. "Further Ado About Negro Music Ability." *Journal of Negro Education* 40 (1971):361–364.

1972

Buegel, Hermann F., and Harris, Jack H. "McCreery Tests of Rhythm and Pitch: Their Reliability and Validity." *Perceptual and Motor Skills* 34 (1972):961–962.

de Troch, Daniel. "Critical Examination of the Conception of the Musical Sense in Experimental Psychology." *Revue de Psychologie et des Sciences de L'Education* 7 (1972):327–344.

Deutsch, Diana. "Octave Generalization and Tune Recognition." *Perception and Psychophysics* 11 (1972):411–412.

Dowling, W. J. "Recognition of Melodic Transformations: Retrograde, and Retrograde Inversion." *Perception and Psychophysics* 12 (1972):417–421.

Fox, J. G., and Embrey, E. D. "Music: An Aid to Productivity." *Applied Ergonomics* 3 (1972):202–205.

Griffin, Lawrence R., and Eisenman, Russell. "Musical Ability and the Drake Music Memory Test." *Educational and Psychological Measurement* 32 (1972):473–476.

Griffin, Lawrence R., and Eisenman, Russell. "Auditory Complexity and Musical Ability." *Perceptual and Motor Skills* 35 (1972):43–46.

Houtsma, A. J., and Goldstein, J. L. "The Central Origin of the Pitch of Complex Tones: Evidence from Musical Interval Recognition." *Journal of the Acoustical Society of America* 51 (1972):520–529.

Irvashita, Toyohiko. "An Experimental Study on the Individual Difference of Affective Meaning Space." *Japanese Journal of Psychology* 43 (1972):188–200.

Irvine, James R., and Kirkpatrick, Walter. "The Musical Form in Rhetorical Exchange: Theoretical Considerations." *Quarterly Journal of Speech* 58 (1972):272–284.

Rintelmann, William F., Lindberg, Robert F., and Smiley, Ellen K. "Temporary Threshold Shift and Recovery Patterns from Two Types of Rock and Roll Music Presentation." *Journal of the Acoustical Society of America* 51 (1972):1249–1255.

Rowe, R. S. and Ivinskis, A. "Melodic Interval Discrimination and the Influence of Training." *Australian Journal of Psychology* 24 (1972):187–192.

Thackray, Rupert. *Rhythmic Abilities in Children.* London: Novello and Company, 1972.

Voledia, A. A. "The Perception of Transient Processes in Musical Sounds." *Voprosy Psikhologic* 18 (1972):51–60.

Wedin, Loge, and Gonde, Gunnar. "Dimension Analysis of the Perception of Instrumental Timbre." *Scandanavian Journal of Psychology* 13 (1972):228–240.

1973

Abeles, Harold F. "Development and Validation of a Clarinet Performance Adjudication Scale." *Journal of Research in Music Education* 21 (1973):246–255.

Bartholomew, Bonnie N., Doehring, Donald G., and Freygood, Steven D. "Absence of Stimulus Effects in Dichotic Singing." *Bulletin of the Psychnomic Society* 1 (1973):171–172.

Bartlett, Dale L. "Effect of Repeated Listenings on Structural Discrimination and Affective Response." *Journal of Research in Music Education* 21 (1973):302–317.

Briscuso, Joseph James. "A Study of Ability in Spontaneous and Prepared Jazz Improvisation Among Students Who Possess Different Levels of Musical Aptitude." *Experimental Research in the Psychology of Music: 9.* Studies in the Psychology of Music, vol. 9. Iowa City: University of Iowa Press, 1973.

Crickmore, Leon. "A Syndrome Hypothesis of Music Appreciation." *Psychology of Music* 1 (1973):21–25.

Foss, Roger V. "An Investigation of the Effect of the Provision of the 'In Doubt' Response on the Validity of the *Iowa Tests of Music Literacy.*" *Experimental Research in the Psychology of Music: 9.* Studies in the Psychology of Music, vol. 9. Iowa City: University of Iowa Press, 1973.

Gordon, Edwin. "Toward the Development of a Taxonomy of Tonal Patterns and Rhythm Patterns: Evidence of Difficulty Level and Growth Rate." *Experimental Research in the Psychology of Music: 9.* Studies in the Psychology of Music, vol. 9. Iowa City: University of Iowa Press, 1973.

Greer, Douglas R., Dorow, Laura, and Hanser, Suzanne. "Music Discrimination Training and the Music Selection Behavior of Nursery and Primary Level Children." *Council for Research in Music Education* 35 (1973):30–43.

Hedden, Steven K. "Listeners' Responses to Music in Relation to Autochthonous and Experimental Factors." *Journal of Research in Music Education* 21 (1973):225–238.

Kantor, Martin, and Pinsker, Henry. "Musical Expression of Psychopathology." *Biology and Medicine* 16 (1973):263–269.

Larson, Ronald L. "Levels of Conceptual Development in Melodic Permutation Concepts Based on Piaget's Theory." *Journal of Research in Music Education* 21 (1973):256–263.

Madsen, Clifford K., and Forsythe, Jere L. "Effect of Contingent Music Listening on Increases of Mathematical Responses." *Journal of Research in Music Education* 21 (1973):176–181.

Meyer, Leonard B. *Explaining Music: Essays and Explorations.* Berkeley: University of California Press, 1973.

Sergeant, Desmond, and Roche, Sheila. "Perceptual Shifts in the Auditory Information Processing of Young Children." *Psychology of Music* 1 (1973):39–48.

Swanwick, Keith. "Musical Cognition and Aesthetic Response." *Psychology of Music* 1 (1973):7–13.

Taylor, Sam. "Musical Development of Children Aged Seven to Eleven." *Psychology of Music* 1 (1973):44–49.

Thackray, Rupert. "Tests of Harmonic Perception." *Psychology of Music* 1 (1973):49–57.

Webster, John C., Woodhead, Muriel M., and Carpenter, Alan. "Perceptual Confusions Between Four-Dimensional Sounds." *Journal of the Acoustical Society of America* 2 (1973):448–456.

Whellams, Frederick S. "Has Musicality a Structure?" *Psychology of Music* 1 (1973):7–9.

Whellams, Frederick S. "Musical Abilities and Sex Differences in the Analysis of Aural-Musical Capacities." *Journal of Research in Music Education* 21 (1973):30–39.

Young, William T. "The Bentley Measures of Musical Abilities: A Congruent Validity Report." *Journal of Research in Music Education* 21 (1973):74–79.

Zuckerkandl, Victor. *Sound and Symbol, Volume 2: Man the Musician.* Trans. by Norbert Guterman. Princeton: Princeton University Press, 1973.

DATE DUE

NOV 3 '76			
Feb 15 '77			
Mar 24 '78G			
May 2 '79 S			
Jun 15 '79 FA			
SEP 5 '79	OCT 1 1 '83 G		
OCT 1 5 PAID			
OCT 2 9 '83 C			
JUN 1 8 '87 S			
AUG 2 3 '91 X			
DEC 1 3 '91			
JAN 3 '94			
JAN 5 PAID			
JUL 27 '98 S			
JUL 2 6 1999			
SEP 02 '08 X			
MAY 2 9 2008			

GAYLORD   PRINTED IN U S A